STUDIES IN HISTORY, ECONOMICS AND PUBLIC LAW

Edited by the

**FACULTY OF POLITICAL SCIENCE
OF COLUMBIA UNIVERSITY**

Number 569

THE FRENCH FRANC BETWEEN THE WARS
1919-1939

BY

MARTIN WOLFE

THE FRENCH FRANC
BETWEEN THE WARS
1919-1939

BY

MARTIN WOLFE

NEW YORK
COLUMBIA UNIVERSITY PRESS
1951

To my father and mother

PREFACE

MONETARY events are woven so tightly into the fabric of modern society that they are not easily isolated. This study is focused on the violent changes in the purchasing power and the exchange value of the French franc; but in tracing the factors behind these changes it has been necessary to go far beyond the fields of money and finance. So many aspects of French political and economic life press for recognition that they have been separated out rather arbitrarily into two sections in each of the central chapters. The first sections present the story chronologically and emphasize the evolution of national monetary policy. The second sections examine more carefully the statistical evidence and discuss pertinent developments in prices, production, balances of trade and payments, income and employment, and the money-market. Readers not wishing to bother with such details may nevertheless be interested in the short concluding statement in each chapter.

While the scope of this study is wide, its pretensions are quite limited. It is not meant to be a treatise on monetary theory or an analysis of various theories in the light of historical experience. Such theoretical elements as are present have been borrowed; of course I alone am responsible for errors committed in their interpretation. The franc has run virtually the whole range of monetary experiences in recent years and provides a rich source for specialists in monetary theory. But first the facts must be known. The object of this book is to help with the work of marshalling these facts into a coherent pattern and thus to explore one of the important strands of French economic history between the wars.

The first ten years of the inter-war history of the franc has been the subject of many excellent monographs, but little has been written on the second decade. The weight of this work, therefore, has been placed on the years 1929-1939. Chapter I contains a brief description of the pre-1914 monetary and financial institutions of France and deals also with the war and immediate post-war years. The main events of the turbulent years 1924-1928 are summarized in Chapter II.

In acknowledging my debts, I should like first of all to express my deep thanks for the patient guidance of Professor Shepard B. Clough and for the privilege of having been a member of his stimulating seminar at Columbia University. The manuscript was greatly strengthened by the friendly criticism of Professor Ragnar Nurkse of Columbia University. Other important suggestions came from Professors Lawrence Seltzer and Sergei Dobrovolsky of Wayne University. The National Bureau of Economic Research allowed me the use of its files. My thanks also go to Columbia University for a University Fellowship in History in the academic year 1947-1948 when I worked in Paris.

One of the bright spots in preparing this study was the courteous and invaluable assistance received from the staff of the Institut scientifique de Recherches économiques et sociales in Paris, and particularly from M. Jean Herberts and M. Charles Rist. I am also grateful for the help given by the librarians at the Institut de science économique appliquée and those at the Ministry of Finance, by Mme. Pirou of UNESCO, M. Moliexe of the Bank of France, and M. Aron of the Banque de Paris et des Pays-Bas. My wife accomplished the usual amount of hard labor thrust upon those unwary enough to marry candidates for higher degrees.

MARTIN WOLFE

WAYNE UNIVERSITY
September, 1950

CONTENTS

CHAPTER IV

CHAPTER V

CHAPTER VI

CHAPTER VII

CHARTS

TABLES

APPENDIXES

CHAPTER I

FRENCH FINANCIAL AND MONETARY INSTITUTIONS TO 1924

THE FINANCIAL AND FISCAL SETTING

LOOKING backward over the past three decades, most Frenchmen old enough to remember the pre-1914 era must think of their recent monetary history as an almost unrelieved series of tragedies. They have seen their currency devalued no less than eight times, often following attacks by speculators who made scandalous profits while the ordinary citizen's savings were wiped out. They have seen their monetary institutions used as the tools of socialist reformers and German conquerors. They have seen their governments experimenting with a freely-fluctuating exchange, with strict exchange control, and with a bewildering variety of currency standards. It is no wonder that a large number of Frenchmen, including some leading economists, are rather despairingly wedded to the concept of stable money.

Today, of course, only a few would suggest seriously that France return to the " good old days " of nineteenth-century financial and monetary institutions. But in 1919, in spite of the shocks suffered by the franc during the First World War, it was universally accepted that the only possible course was to reëstablish the pre-war monetary system as quickly as possible. For generations specie-based currency and " sane " financial policies had been associated with stability and prosperity. Until 1926 the whole frame of reference of the makers of monetary policy was the pre-1914 paradise which must somehow be regained.

The French franc before 1914.—The great symbol of this pre-war monetary paradise was the franc itself. Established by the law of *7 Germinal an XI* (March 28, 1803), the franc was defined as five grams of silver nine-tenths fine (or the equivalent value of gold at the ratio of one part of gold to 15.5 parts of silver) and remained so for 125 years. This bimetallic system was modified in 1865, however, when, with the rest of the Latin Monetary Union, France withdrew the right of free coinage for the smaller silver coins. In 1878 free coinage of the five-franc silver *écu* was denied, and France in effect went on the gold standard. Since silver coins continued to circulate, however, and since they possessed full legal tender power, France had what is known as a "limping" bimetallic standard.[1]

For her paper money France relied exclusively on notes printed by the Bank of France, which institution had retained the monopoly of bank-note issue ever since 1803. So great was the confidence enjoyed by the Bank that until 1928, alone of all the world's great banks of issue, it was not required to back its notes by any legally-fixed percentage of specie. It was a source of great pride to the Bank that apart from the crisis years 1848-1849 and 1870-1873 it had never been forced to suspend specie convertibility for its bank-notes.[2]

The règle du plafond.—Before 1848, and between 1850 and 1870, in fact, there was no legal limitation whatsoever on either the quantity or the quality of bank-notes in circulation; this matter was left entirely to the discretion of the Bank's directors. But after the resumption of full specie convertibility in 1878, the "rule of the ceiling" (*règle du plafond*) was retained, by which the legislature set a maximum for bank-notes in circulation. Fixed originally at 2.8 billion francs, the "ceiling" was raised by stages until, at the occasion of the last pre-war renewal of the Bank's charter (1911), it was brought up to 6.8 billions.

Until 1928, therefore, when a new monetary law required a fixed percentage of precious metals to be kept in reserve against

1 Gaëtan Pirou, *Traité d'économie politique*, vol. II, *Le Mécanisme de la vie économique: La Monnaie* (Paris: Recueil Sirey, 1945), pp. 60-65.

2 After 1873, however, convertibility was restored only gradually; it was not until 1878 that all denominations of banknotes were convertible. Gabriel Ramon, *Histoire de la Banque de France* (Paris: Bernard Grasset, 1929), p. 385.

bank-notes in circulation,[3] the Bank of France remained unique among banks of issue in that the only legal control over its notes was the *plafond*. There was no law preventing the Bank from squandering its gold and silver reserves to the point where it would not be able to redeem its notes in precious metals. On the other hand, there was nothing to prevent the French government from demanding dangerously large loans from the Bank of France, since the *plafond* could be raised by majority vote of the legislature. Between 1924 and 1926 a struggle developed between the government and the Bank on this point; the government found it necessary to demand large sums of money to meet Treasury deficits, while the Bank fought to limit the inflationary activities of the government.

The role of the Bank of France.[4]—It would be difficult to exaggerate the importance to the French economy of the Bank of France since its organization by Napoleon in 1800. The function of bank of issue was only one of many it performed. It was also the fiscal agent of the State, a central bank of rediscount, and the largest commercial bank in France, with more than six hundred branch offices and agencies in all but the most insignificant hamlets in the country. As a commercial bank, it discounted bills up to ninety days' maturity with two or three endorsements, depending on the security offered, and made loans on French and foreign securities and gold. As a bankers' bank, the Bank of France had a certain amount of control over the money-market through the discount and rediscount rates; until 1936, however, the Bank did not seek the authority to control fluctuations in credit by " open-market " operations (buying and selling short-term government securities and commercial bills) because it was believed this would constitute an interference with the " automatic " functioning of the gold standard and might prove inflationary.[5] As a fiscal agent, the

3 See chapter II.

4 For a discussion of the administration of the Bank and its changes in 1936, see chapter V.

5 Margaret Myers, *Paris as a Financial Center* (New York: Columbia University Press, 1936), pp. 30-31. See also Pirou, *op. cit.*, pp. 337-338.

Bank accepted government revenues for deposit, handled inter-governmental payments, helped in the distribution of bond issues, and could be called upon in times of Treasury deficits to advance " extraordinary " loans to the government.

The French banking system.—The complex of French bank-ing institutions could hardly be called a " system." [6] The banks in France were characterized by amazing variety and complete absence of public control. Besides the commercial banking activities of the central bank, there were the powerful " Big Four," joint-stock commercial banks, each with hundreds of branch offices, which handled the bulk of the short-term trade advances. There were also joint-stock banks which specialized in industrial loans, the mortgage business, and colonial trade. The important *banques d'affaires* were exceptions in that they were non-specialized, " mixing " the functions of deposit and commercial banking and securities investment. In the " pri-vate " sector were the French banks owned by the great finan-cial families; these included the famous " Maisons de Haute banque," which dealt in long-term investments, especially in government securities, and the bankers and agents dealing on the Bourse. Finally, there was a bewildering array of public and " semi-public " banking establishments: those for munici-pal and agricultural loans, the important public savings banks system, the " Bank for deposits and funds in litigation " (*Caisse des dépôts et consignations*), the postal savings system, and the *Crédit National,* originally organized to manage the loans for post-war (1918) reconstruction.[7] The Treasury itself accepted savings deposits under certain conditions.[8]

Even the number of banks in France was unknown. In 1927, for example, there were 256 incorporated banks which filed tax reports, but at the same time there were more than 150 un-

---

6 *Ibid.,* p. 100.

7 The best systematization of the French banking complex is in Henry Laufenburger, *Les Banques françaises* (Paris: Recueil Sirey, 1940), pp. 15-22 and *passim.*

8 After December, 1920.

incorporated banks of various descriptions operating in Paris alone.[9]

Another striking characteristic of the privately owned and joint-stock banks in France was their independence of public control. In strange contrast to the banking system of the United States, the great commercial banks of France operated without any legal reserve requirements against deposits, and with no governmental inspectors or insurance agents to enforce adherence to generally-accepted banking principles. There were no special incorporation laws for banks. The powerful commercial banks usually could ignore the discount and rediscount rates established by the Bank of France in considering the advisability of advancing credit.[10] They were not required to publish periodical statements, and in fact could conduct their business in strictest privacy. As a result, neither the minister of finance nor the governor of the Bank nor anybody else had a complete picture of French financial life. The large banks did publish statements sporadically, but the statistics furnished were not very useful, since their bases varied from bank to bank and from time to time.

Involved with his suspicion of the motives of prying statisticians was the Frenchman's distrust of checks; checks require signatures and contain financial information which might be of interest to the tax collector. Most payments in France except the very largest, in fact, were—and are—made in cash or postal transfers. Aside from his characteristic preference for " real " money, there were objective reasons why a Frenchman avoided checks: under French law the drawer and drawee were insufficiently protected, and there was also a slight but annoying tax (50 *centimes* in 1933) on each check cashed.[11]

9 Myers, *op. cit.*, p. 100. For the year 1936 Laufenburger counts 199 unincorporated banks publishing reports, 731 other joint-stock banks, and a grand total of 2,106 banks of all descriptions. Laufenburger, *op. cit.*, pp. 20-22.

10 *Ibid.*, p. 347.

11 Myers, *op. cit.*, pp. 128-130.

The whole concept of " money in circulation " was radically different in France from that in the United States or in Great Britain. In the latter two countries money in circulation was usually regarded as being roughly equivalent to coins and paper money outside the banking system, plus demand deposits, with the latter category by far the most important. In the United States about 90 per cent of all commercial transactions in 1935 were made by check. The ratio of all deposits—both demand and time deposits—to currency in the United States was about twenty to one; in France the same ratio was only three to two.[12] In France currency in circulation amounted to about 35 per cent of the national income in 1938, while in the same year the ratio was only about 10 per cent in the United States.

The general characteristics of demand deposits in the " Big Four " French banks were quite different from those in our country. The French deposits were not primarily connected to loans to commerce and industry; they were regarded by French firms as a sort of secondary outlet for reserve funds. This accounts for the tendency of French *dépôts à vue* to shrink during prosperity and to swell in times of depression when idle funds are abundant.[13]

Finally the manner in which French banks handled their reports on deposits presents difficulties of analysis which are statistically insurmountable. On the credit side of the ledger, the column " commercial portfolio " usually included the short-term government bonds discounted,[14] and on the debit side the column " current accounts and sight deposits " included too many types of liabilities to be useful.[15] More complete infor-

12 *Ibid.*, pp. 131-132.

13 James H. Rogers, *The Process of Inflation in France, 1914-1927* (New York: Columbia University Press, 1929), pp. 301-303.

14 Gaëtan Pirou, *Cours d'économie politique* (Paris: Domat-Montchrestien, 1947), I, 335 ff.

15 Myers, *op. cit.*, p. 51.

mation on deposits, the French banks—including the Bank of France—could not or would not give.[16]

Paris as a financial center.—Paris had never succeeded in developing an international money-market comparable to that of London or New York. Most of the trading in the Parisian money-market consisted of long-term securities more properly regarded as investments. It was impossible, moreover, to separate the money-market proper from the banks. There were few special foreign bill brokers or acceptance houses; an attempt to start an acceptance house failed during the depression of the 1930's.[17] When the need for short-term bills arose, they could easily be obtained from near-by London. The banks concerned with the money-market were not clustered in any one area of Paris; they were jealous of their prerogatives and would not cooperate with each other or with the Bank of France, thus depriving the Paris financial center of both control and " leadership." [18] Even governmental agencies such as the Treasury and the *Caisse des dépôts et consignations* at times acted at cross-purposes.[19]

The inter-bellum decades saw a decline in the importance of the Paris money-market due to the growth of " self-financing." The wartime and post-war inflation and the period of prosperity after 1927 enabled the larger institutionalized corporations to break out of debt and build up their own reserve funds, thus reducing the volume of *beau papier* (high-grade negotiable

16 Rogers, *op. cit.*, p. 162. For all these reasons, in this study changes in bank deposits are considered as corroborative evidence only.

17 Laufenburger, *op. cit.*, pp. 317-318.

18 *La France économique en 1925, annuaire de la vie économique française,* annual publication of the *Revue d'économie politique* (Paris: Recueil Sirey), p. 299. Two separate paginations can be found for *La France économique,* since it is published both as a separate monograph (beginning in 1927) and as one of the regular numbers of the *Revue d'économie politique* (beginning in 1922). The page references in this study are to the latter edition.

19 Myers, *op. cit.*, pp. 66, 90.

bills) in France. With the immense growth of the " floating " public debt, government short-term bonds (*bons de la défense nationale* and *bons ordinaires du Trésor*) became the standard medium of short-term operations rather than commercial paper, but even these bonds were absorbed to a large extent by the public sector of the banking system, especially by the savings banks and the *Caisse des dépôts et consignations.*[20] Because these short-term *bons* provided the French banks with an outlet for surplus cash, they lessened the necessity for an integrated money-market in Paris.[21]

French taxes and the war.—The foregoing general description of French financial institutions has emphasized their inadequacies; until 1914, however, contemporary opinion rated France's financial system as second only to England's. The pre-war decades were fairly comfortable ones, years of prosperity and stability. The French banks, and particularly the Bank of France, were everywhere respected for their " strength," evidenced by the large amounts of gold in their coffers. The " automatic " gold standard seemed to be fulfilling all the claims of its proponents by providing a sound money. Even after the burdens of war and reconstruction had demonstrated the weakness in the French monetary and financial structure, most Frenchmen continued to regard the pre-war situation as the " normalcy " which must be regained at all cost.

The pre-1914 tax structure was regarded with less complacency. The Frenchman was a self-admitted grudging taxpayer, unwilling to pay for the public services he demanded.[22] His main requirement for good taxes was that they be so ancient that, like old shoes, they would not pinch. The basis of

20 Laufenburger, *op. cit.*, pp. 336-343.

21 Rogers, *op. cit.*, pp. 27-29.

22 Louis Trotabas, *Les Finances publiques et les impôts de la France* (Paris: Armand Colin, 1937), p. 15. See also Gaston Jèze and Henri Truchy, *The War Finance of France* (" Economic and Social History of the War," Carnegie Endowment for International Peace; New Haven: Yale University Press, 1927), p. 187.

direct taxation in 1914 was still the *quatre vieilles contributions,* originating in the tax laws of 1791. All of these " four old ladies " (*quatre vieilles*), as they appropriately came to be called, were based on " external signs," a slogan dear to the hearts of Frenchmen, who have always been extremely reluctant to divulge financial information. One of the *quatre vieilles* was the *impôt des portes et des fenêtres,* literally a tax on doors and windows; a taxpayer was assessed according to these features of his home, which were taken as an indication of his wealth.[23] This quaint method of assessing wealth has been called a carry-over from Revolutionary attitudes toward tax collectors,[24] and remains a serious stumbling-block in the path of efforts for fiscal reform to this day.[25]

Tied up with this insistence on the sacrosanct nature of private business was the strong French propensity to hoard. Like the banker, both the close-fisted French peasant and the *rentier* were most reluctant to give information which, for all they knew, might some day be used against them. As a result, tax evasion was—and remains—a serious problem.[26] Every inter-bellum budgetary crisis brought out a rash of laws aimed at fiscal fraud, all powerless to change the habits of centuries. Tax reform is difficult ". . . in a country which considers the inviolability of domestic secrecy to be an essential form of liberty." [27]

23 The other three were the *impôt foncier* (land tax), the *impôt personnel-mobilier* (property tax), and the *impôt des patentes* (license tax).

24 Sir George Peel, *The Financial Crisis of France* (London: Macmillan Co., 1925), p. 52.

25 New tax laws passed in the winter of 1947-1948 included the provision that one of the methods for determining the income tax payable by an individual was to ascertain the number of servants he employed and the number of automobiles he possessed.

26 All French *bons* and *rentes* are exempt by law from special taxes; the income received as interest on securities, on the other hand, is taxable as such. But the French government has found that the only way it can sell its bonds and Treasury bills is to take no record of the names of purchasers nor of amounts purchased. (*New York Times,* Feb. 6, 1949.)

27 Georges Lachapelle, *Les Finances de la Troisième République* (Paris: Flammarion, 1937), p. 65.

Serious attempts to reform the French tax system in the pre-war period began in 1907 when the finance minister, Caillaux, proposed the substitution of an income tax for the " quatre vieilles." According to his plan, incomes would be classified into " schedules " based on the source of income, with different tax rates applied to each " schedule" (*impôt cédulaire*). Over all income, no matter what the source, a general progressive tax rate would be fixed (*impôt général*). Incomes would be declared in writing to tax controllers, and failure to declare properly would be punishable by fines.[28]

This proposal became a parliamentary whipping-post for more than seven years, in spite of the pleas of its advocates that an income tax was a precondition of adequate national defense. Roundly denounced as " inquisitorial," the bill was referred to the Chamber's finance committee, which debated the proposal for two long years, removed several " schedules," and increased general exemptions. Then the bill went to the Senate, and that body required five more years to agree to an even more emasculated version of Caillaux's original proposal. The French income tax was finally approved in this form on July 15, 1914, but its application was postponed until December, 1915, when it was arranged that it would take effect in 1916. This law set a flat 2 per cent rate, involved no obligatory declaration of income, and did not even replace the old direct taxes. " It was little more than an experiment." [29] In 1914, therefore, France found herself with an antiquated, patched-up tax system, entirely inadequate to the tremendous burden of the war.

Very few other tax improvements were made during the war. In July, 1916 a war profits tax of 50 per cent on profits over 6 per cent was imposed; in July, 1917 the Caillaux income tax by schedules was finally substituted for the old system

28 Robert M. Haig, *The Public Finances of Post-War France* (New York: Columbia University Press, 1929), p. 50.

29 Jèze and Truchy, *op. cit.*, pp. 188, 204 ff.

of direct taxes; [30] and in December, 1917 a 10 per cent tax was levied on all luxury goods. In 1918 there were some further slight increases in indirect taxation, particularly on sugar and tobacco.[31] These half-hearted measures did not begin to pay for the gigantic expenses of the war; [32] in terms of prices and wages French tax revenue probably shrank during the war years. The rest of the necessary funds were obtained by borrowing from the Bank of France in the form of " extraordinary advances " and from the French public in the form of *bons de la défense nationale,* Treasury bonds, and four important issues of *rentes.*

TABLE 1
FRENCH TAX REVENUE DURING THE WAR *

	Billions of Francs	Wholesale Price Index July, 1914 = 100 (Average for the Year)	Salary Index of a Lower-Grade *Fonctionnaire* (Letter Carrier) 1914 = 100	(2) ÷ (3)	(2) ÷ (4)
(1)	(2)	(3)	(4)	(5)	(6)
1913	5.1	...	...	..	..
1914	4.6	104	100	4.4	4.6
1915	4.1	143	145	2.9	2.8
1916	5.2	192	200	2.7	2.6
1917	6.9	267	235	2.6	2.9
1918	7.6	346	280	2.2	2.5
1919	13.3	364	325	3.7	4.1

* Source: *Inventaire:* (2), p. 230; (3), p. 223; (4), p. 348.

30 The shift from one system of direct taxes to another resulted in a *loss* of thirty-two million francs in tax revenues in 1917. *Ibid.,* p. 201.

31 Haig, *op. cit.,* p. 40.

32 The true monetary cost of the First World War to France (apart from reconstruction costs) is not known; in all probability it never will be known. See Jèze and Truchy, *op. cit.,* p. 105. The sum suggested by Truchy for all government expenditures 1914-1919 is 210 billion francs (current value) ; *ibid.,* p. 193. A later French estimate of all government expenditures 1914-1919 is only 176.4 billion francs. See Ministère des Finances, *Inventaire de la situation financière (1913-1946)* (Paris: Imprimerie Nationale, 1946), p. 595. In addition, France spent about 156 billion francs for reconstruction.

A complicating factor in the fiscal picture was the occupation of an important sector of industrial France by the enemy. Although only 4 per cent of metropolitan France was under German control, the occupied area had accounted for more than 20 per cent of France's internal revenue, not to mention 70 per cent of her coal, 63 per cent of her steel, and 78 per cent of her beet sugar. Yet another reduction in revenue was represented by a law allowing families of men in service to be excused from paying direct taxes.[33]

Part of the explanation for the failure of the French fiscal system to be revised in any important manner until 1916 lies in the political situation in France at the beginning of the war. During 1914 and most of 1915 the French administration kept the legislature in a completely subordinate role; however justifiable this may or may not have been from the point of view of the actual conduct of the war, it allowed Alexandre Ribot, the conservative Minister of Finance, to ignore any suggestions for fiscal reform. It was the announced policy of the government during 1914 and 1915 to avoid recourse to additional sources of taxation, so as not to aggravate the burdens laid on the country by the war.[34] Moreover, the unselective mass mobilization in the first days of the war completely disrupted the technical services of the Ministry of Finance, as it did the entire public and private financial apparatus of France; from the beginning of the war through 1923 nobody in France had any precise notion of governmental receipts and expenditures.[35] The weak position of the government in fiscal matters was used by the opposition parties in the legislature in eventually (October, 1915) causing the fall of the Viviani ministry.[36] Even with the change in fiscal policy that came with the new govern-

33 Peel, *The Economic Policy of France* (London: Macmillan Co., 1937), p. 111.

34 Jèze and Truchy, *op. cit.*, pp. 196-197.

35 *Ibid.*, pp. 27-40.

36 Haig, *op. cit.*, pp. 26-27.

ment, the tax laws of 1916, 1917, and 1918 resulted in increases in tax revenue of only 4.5 billion francs, inconsiderable in view of the 176 billions borrowed by the French State during the war.[37]

THE FRANC DURING WAR AND RECONSTRUCTION

At the outset of the First World War few could imagine that four years of havoc lay ahead. In France and elsewhere most people thought that a war of such intensity could last three or four months at the most.[38] The French franc was expected to weather the storm; at times foreign exchange markets actually quoted the franc at above par.[39] Although the Bank of France suspended gold convertibility and the government forbade gold exports soon after the opening of hostilities, confidence in the permanence and inviolability of France's monetary system was such that exchange control was not imposed on the country until 1916.

Meanwhile the exigencies of total war were reducing drastically the amount of non-military production in France. In 1918, just after the war, French industry was at 60 per cent of its 1913 level. Agricultural production had fallen to 70 per cent of the 1913 total.[40] But currency in circulation was rising rapidly at the same time; prices in France responded quickly to a huge " inflationary gap."

The process of inflation in France.—A strong upward pressure on prices resulted from the great extent to which France turned to " extraordinary " advances from the Bank of France

37 The true total borrowing of the French State during the war may be as much as thirty billion francs higher than this figure. See Shepard B. Clough, *France, A History of National Economics, 1789-1939* (New York: Charles Scribner's Sons, 1939), p. 266.

38 Etienne Clémentel, *La France et la politique économique interalliée* (Paris: Presses Universitaires, 1931), p. 2.

39 Paul Einzig, *Exchange Control* (London: Macmillan Co., 1934), p. 23. See also Eleanor L. Dulles, *The French Franc, 1914-1928* (New York: Macmillan Co., 1929), p. 103.

40 Clough, *op. cit.*, pp. 292-293.

to pay the costs of war. The first of these advances was in fulfillment of a secret convention of November 30, 1911, that in
case of mobilization for war the Bank would loan an additional
2.9 billion francs to the French Treasury.[41] After the declaration of war, the *plafond* was raised from 6.8 to 12 billion
francs and then, by successive stages, to 41 billions in September, 1920.

From December, 1913 to December, 1920 total bank-notes in
circulation rose from 5.7 to 37.9 billion francs.[42] This tremendous increase of 32.2 billion francs [43] was vastly beyond the
needs of business expansion in wartime France; it was rather
the result of the 25.6 billions of " extraordinary " advances to
the State.[44]

First appearance of exchange depreciation.—When it became evident that the war was to be a matter of many destruc-
tive years rather than a few short months, confidence in the
franc began to sag. Fearing the effect of high prices on the exchange rate of the franc, investors began to transfer some of
their funds to London or New York. In 1915 the French government urged banks to deny foreign exchange to suspected
speculators; [45] the minister of finance announced that this de-
sertion of the franc in time of war was an affair of national
honor.[46] But increasing demand for British and American exchange continued the alarming downward pressure on the

41 Pirou, *La Monnaie française depuis la guerre, 1914-1936* (Paris:
Recueil Sirey, 1936), p. 19.

42 *Inventaire*, p. 595. Increases in bank deposits did not play an important
part in French wartime inflation. Most French banks made loans more
cautiously than ever, and actually increased the ratio of their reserves to
their liabilities. See Clémentel, *op. cit.*, p. 7.

43 Partially offset by the virtual disappearance of six billions in gold and
silver coins through hoarding, export, or patriotic sale to the government.
See Pirou, *Traité*, p. 165.

44 Rogers, *op. cit.*, p. 55.

45 Jèze and Truchy, *op. cit.*, pp. 295-296.

46 Einzig, *op. cit.*, p. 24.

franc, and in 1916 the government decided to intervene. The Treasury made arrangements with New York and London banking houses to buy up all French bills, notes, or securities offered at a rate lower than 19.31 cents per franc (about 5.18 francs per dollar). The money necessary for these " pegging " operations was provided by the French Treasury.[47] Thanks to currency agreements among France, the United Kingdom, and the United States, the Bank of France was able to provide French importers with foreign exchange at about pre-war par rates.[48]

During the war, then, the exchange value of the franc was maintained at just about par, in spite of the vast increase in currency in circulation, in spite of the fact that the franc's purchasing power in France was steadily dropping, and in spite of a heavily unfavorable balance of payments due to purchases of the necessities of war.[49]

TABLE 2

WARTIME INFLATION IN FRANCE *

(1)	Bank-Note Circulation (billions of francs) (2)	Wholesale Price Index (1913 = 100) (3)	Retail Price Index (1914 = 100) (4)	Dollar Rate in Paris (francs) (5)
1913	5.8	100	...	5.16
1914	10.0	113	100	5.17
1915	13.3	167	120	5.85
1916	16.7	208	138	5.84
1917	22.3	279	184	5.70
1918	30.2	360	237	5.45

* Sources: Dulles, *op. cit.*, (2), p. 481; (3), p. 510; (4), p. 511; Rogers, *op. cit.*, (5), p. 59. All figures are for the end of the year.

47 In this country these stabilizing activities were taken over by the United States Treasury after we entered the war.

48 Dulles, *op. cit.*, p. 104.

49 France's unfavorable balance of commodity trade rose from 1.5 billion francs in 1914 to 23.9 billions in 1919; the total for 1914-1919 was 86.1 billion francs. See Frank A. Haight, *A History of French Commercial Policies* (New York: Macmillan Co., 1944), p. 88.

With the cessation of hostilities, inter-Allied economic co-operation ended abruptly and with it the " pegging " operations which had held the exchange rate of the franc steady at its pre-war level. The dollar rate in Paris shot up from 5.45 to 10.87 francs during 1919 and reached 16.80 francs at the end of 1920.[50] But instead of either trying to stabilize the franc at some exchange level commensurate with its reduced purchasing power in France or instituting exchange control, the govern-ment and the Bank of France, with a remarkable display of faith, assumed that the franc would somehow regain its pre-war par value, and that when this was achieved the gold stand-ard would be restored. Had not the dollar been retained at its pre-war gold parity? Was not the Bank of England now en-gaged in a campaign for deflation to restore pre-war gold parity to the pound sterling? France, which was after all one of the victors in the late struggle, must help the franc " look the pound and the dollar in the face " by restoring its full value in terms of gold and foreign exchange.[51]

Because of the world's esteem for France's financial and monetary institutions, the French were not alone in believing that the pre-war parity of the franc would be restored. In 1919 and 1920, in fact, each further depreciation of the franc brought in a wave of speculators who bought francs " cheap " with ex-pectations of future profits; their dealings helped to hold up the exchange rate of the franc and of other depreciating Continen-tal currencies.[52] This tendency was temporarily reinforced by the drop of prices inside France which accompanied the post-war depression of 1920-1921. During 1921 the dollar in Paris fell from 16.80 to 13.14 francs, and continued to fall, reaching 10.90 francs in April, 1922.[53]

50 *Bulletin de la Statistique Générale de la France et du Service d'obser-vation des prix* (Paris: Librairie Felix Alcan). (Hereinafter referred to as " SGF.")

51 Pirou, *Traité*, p. 218.

52 League of Nations, *International Currency Experiences* (Princeton: Princeton University Press, 1944), p. 113.

53 *SGF.*

From the beginning of the war, the French government had taken the position that the vast increase of the circulating media of exchange must be regarded as a temporary phenomenon.[54] On April 20, 1920 the "François-Marsal Convention" was drawn up between the Bank and the government, providing that the Treasury should repay each year, beginning in 1921, two billion francs of its loans from the Bank of France, until these "extraordinary" advances were wiped out.[55] It was confidently expected that this measure would restore the franc to its 1914 exchange value. Very little thought was given to the fact that, by contracting money in circulation and driving down the French price level, repayment of these advances would represent a crushing increase in the real value of the interest paid on the internal national debt. Not until the German experience of hyper-inflation and the "attack on the franc" in 1924 [56] did many people seriously entertain doubts that "a franc is a franc."

The "phantom of reparations."—The problem of huge expenditures and resulting deficits did not end in 1918. There was still the cost of reconstruction to be met, and France energetically attacked the problem of rebuilding the devastated *départements*. During the war France had promised her citizens that they would not have to bear the costs of property losses due to war damage. Besides financing the reconstruction of private dwellings, the Ministry of Public Works undertook the replacement and repair of damaged roads, bridges, and public buildings. Expenditures on reconstruction from 1919 to 1926, when the job was practically finished, resulted in budgets that were as large as or larger than those of the war years.[57]

54 Pirou, *Traité*, p. 164.

55 Lachapelle, *op. cit.*, pp. 102-103. These payments were met only once —in December, 1921.

56 See chapter II.

57 As a result of the price inflation after 1921, however, these budgets were smaller in terms of *Germinal* francs than those of the war years.

Tax receipts did not begin to pay the costs of reconstruction, and the government continued its wartime policy of borrowing. In addition to its usual sources of loans, the government set up a special agency to finance the cost of reconstruction: the *Crédit National pour faciliter la réparation des dommages causés par la guerre.* This was an association of the principal banks in France, issuing bonds guaranteed by the Treasury. Between 1919 and 1924 the *Crédit National* floated eight large loans.

Under the pressure of the huge war and reconstruction expenditures, the French national debt climbed from 173 billion francs in 1918 to 428 billions in 1924. At first the French were not too uneasy about this development. Let Germany pay! was the general feeling. Let Germany pay for the war damage, as she had forced France to pay after the Franco-Prussian War. The ministers of finance repeatedly announced that in floating the heavy loans for reconstruction France was merely acting as Germany's "banker," and that the costs would have to be borne eventually by the German people. Thus was created the " phantom of reparations " which was to haunt the French for the next decade.

This complacent attitude was reflected in the structure of the French budgets. Besides the regular *budget ordinaire,* there were the *budget extraordinaire,* born of wartime needs, and the *budget des dépenses recouvrables.*[58] This last budget involved the loans of the *Crédit National,* eventually to be " recovered " from Germany as reparations. By presenting the *budget ordinaire* as being " balanced " by taxation and the others as the concern of the future, this system of multiple accounting engendered a baseless complacency in the budgetary situation.

In 1921 the French government submitted a report to the Reparation Commission claiming damages of 218 billion

---

58 The picture was further complicated by the existence of *budgets annexes, budgets autonomes, comptes hors budgets,* and *comptes spéciaux.* See Trotabas, *op. cit.,* pp. 44-46. See also Peel, *The Economic Policy of France,* p. 69.

francs.[59] This immense sum was entirely beyond the ability of Germany to pay without disrupting her economy, which had been seriously strained as a result of the war. The situation was complicated by the refusal of the French government to accept all that Germany was ready to offer in the way of reparations " in kind." [60] In June, 1922 discussions of the Reparation Commission at Geneva broke down when Great Britain and the United States decided that the German mark, faced by prospects of runaway inflation, should be put on a sounder basis before Germany paid further reparations.[61] The exchange depreciation of the franc immediately assumed serious proportions. Under pressure of a wave of pessimism concerning reparations, the rate of the dollar in Paris, which previously (April, 1922) had declined to 10.90 francs, now rose sharply to 13.84 francs in December, and to 16.28 francs in February, 1923.[62] Desperate, the French government sent an army into the German Ruhr in January, 1923 and announced that it was there to stay until the Germans paid up. This dramatic stroke touched off a campaign of " passive resistance " by the German government with the fervent support of the German people. The expenses of occupation virtually cancelled out the profits made by the French by their control of Ruhr industry. And the separation of the Ruhr from the rest of the German economy proved fatal for the already-weakening German mark. In October, 1923 the German government indicated its willingness to resume reparations payments, and the Dawes Committee began

59 The maximum allowable to France under the Versailles Treaty was much less. See Jèze and Truchy, *op. cit.*, pp. 79-90.

60 During the year 1922 Germany had offered France goods and services to the value of 800 million gold marks in reparations; the French government, perhaps under pressure by French business interests to prevent German competition, accepted only 200 million gold marks "in kind." *La France économique en 1922*, pp. 139-140.

61 France had already received about four billion francs (1928 value) from Germany as reparations.

62 *SGF*.

its work of reëstablishing German monetary stability and drawing up a feasible plan for reparations.

After the acceptance of the Dawes Report by the Reparation Commission and by Germany, the French began the withdrawal of their occupation forces from the Ruhr, greatly to the relief of the consciences of liberally-minded Frenchmen. The disastrous episode had proved beyond a doubt that the French could not expect miracles in the way of reparations from Germany. The average Frenchman slowly began to realize that, in one way or another, he, and not the Germans, would have to bear most of the cost of the war to France.[63]

> As a taxpayer, he would have to take up his loss as a bondholder. For practically every thousand francs that the Germans did not pay, he, as a taxpayer, would have to pass a thousand-franc note from one trouser-pocket to the other, and then, as a bondholder, tear up one of his thousand-franc *bons,* replacing it with his tax receipt. Thus to commit financial hara-kiri was certainly not his conception of the role of a conqueror. Had he defeated the Germans only to be robbed by them? . . . The individual Frenchman became sickeningly conscious that, if Germany did not pay, his personal fortunes were ruined.[64]

63 Under the Dawes and Young plans, France continued to receive reparations from Germany until 1931; between 1924 and 1931 France received the equivalent of 1.4 billion dollars from Germany, or about 35.6 billion "Poincaré francs." By the end of 1927, on the other hand, France had expended 130.2 billion francs (current value) in reconstruction, and some 26 billions in private claims still remained to be met. Haig, *op. cit.,* p. 304.

64 *Ibid.,* p. 29.

CHAPTER II
THE FOUR-SOU FRANC

The End of the Germinal Franc

The collapse of the Ruhr occupation was followed by a sudden collapse in the dreams of the French for full and immediate settlement of their monetary difficulties by German reparations. This bitter awakening lent a new and frightening significance to the rise in prices in France and the drop in the exchange value of the franc which had followed the war. But inflation and depreciation were complicated by the inability or unwillingness of the French legislature and governments to recognize the new state of monetary affairs and to take steps to stabilize the franc on a lower level. During a long, frustrating period of useless bickering and stalemates, confidence in the franc dropped so low that on two separate occasions France teetered on the edge of hyper-inflation.

The " attack on the franc."—The first of these occasions has come to be known as the " attack on the franc." The " attack " developed in the winter of 1923-1924 as an attempt by professional speculators in France and abroad to take advantage of the shaky situation in the Bourse and on the French political scene. A wave of " short-selling " brought the franc from about six cents down to four cents in less than three months, and a great outcry was raised against these " hostile " speculators who were plotting the downfall of France. In the Chamber Poincaré charged that the offensive against the franc was directed " at least as much at political as at financial ends "; he cited a report from a French consul in Germany that German financial concerns were advising clients to sell holdings in francs as quickly as possible to help themselves and to help Germany.[1] The movement soon gained the proportions of a

---

1 *Journal Officiel, Débats Parlementaires, Chambre des Députés* (Paris: Imprimerie Nationale, 1924), p. 321. One authority believes that it is possible that the "attack on the franc" was touched off by speculators in Germany and Austria, who took advantage of the situation to strike at their "enemy"

panic when the eighth loan of the *Crédit National* failed, still further shaking public confidence in the government's ability to pay. In January the Bank of France raised its discount rate from 5 to 6 per cent in an attempt to cut down on the amount of funds available to speculators; this classic maneuver was, as usual, too late to stop "hostile" speculation, since the profits to be made on "selling short" far outweighed the slightly increased cost of borrowing funds. Rather the effect was actually the reverse of that desired; the raising of the discount rate was interpreted as a sign of weakness on the part of the Bank of France and the Treasury. Government attempts to help the situation by removing foreigners from the Bourse and by threatening court action against speculators also backfired, merely aggravating the panic. Amid shouts that he was needlessly frightening the country, Maurice Bokanowski, *rapporteur* of the Chamber's Finance Commission, stated that:

> The day of January 14, when the dollar rose from 21 to 23.3 francs and the pound sterling from 90 to 98 francs, caused us, I repeat, an anguish similar to that we experienced when the front at Chemin-des-Dames was broken through. The monetary defenses of France seemed to be pierced; all its substance could have leaked out through the break.[2]

In March, 1924 a new *Bloc National* government was formed under Raymond Poincaré, pledged to save the franc at all costs. A radical tax bill giving the government authority to

---

by dumping francs on the sagging money-market. Dulles, *op. cit.*, pp. 170-171. But Lord Keynes, an observer of this "attack," wrote that to attribute it to political vengeance was "like blaming sickness on the evil eye." Quoted in André Bouton, *La Fin des rentiers* (Paris: Editions M.-P. Trémois, 1930), p. 131. In an interview with the present writer (April 22, 1948) Charles Rist, now Honorary Governor of the Bank of France and one of France's chief financial experts, said that the men who made this "attack" were much more interested in the speculative profits involved than in striking at France.

2 *JO, Chambre, Débats*, 1924, p. 274.

increase all taxes 20 per cent was jammed through the Chamber of Deputies (the " double décime "), coupled with a cut of more than a billion francs in government expenditures. On the basis of this very evident determination to straighten out the French fiscal tangle, Poincaré was able to negotiate a secret loan of four million pounds sterling from Lazard Frères in London and another of one hundred million dollars from Morgan and Company in New York. The proceeds of these loans were suddenly thrown on the market in a dramatic attempt to " squeeze the bears." Sudden heavy buying in the face of previous speculative selling forced up the market rate on francs very rapidly; many fortunes made during the " attack on the franc " were as suddenly lost, resulting in a sizeable flurry of bankruptcy and suicide.[3] The franc rose from an average of 4.68 cents in March to 6.16 cents in April.

Continued financial indecision.—The general elections of May, 1924 resulted in a defeat for the *Bloc National* and, therefore, for Poincaré. The *Cartel des Gauches,* a union of Socialists and Radical-Socialists, emerged victorious. The new premier was Edouard Herriot. Although the Socialist party refused to allow any of its members to be compromised by accepting a ministerial post, the upper bourgeoisie generally regarded the new government as radical and untrustworthy. None of the *Cartel* financial proposals was passed by the Senate. The " double décime " never went into operation, and the government continued to borrow heavily.

The end of the Herriot régime came in April, 1925, when the *rapporteur* of the Senate's finance commission substantiated the rumors that the government had forced the Bank of France to " break through the ceiling " limiting bank-note issue. Herriot's excuse was that the State had been relying on similar practices ever since 1920.[4] Previous governments had persuaded large private banks to loan the Treasury money when the legal

---

3 Bouton, *op. cit.*, pp. 133-134.

4 *JO, Sénat, Débats,* 1925, pp. 842-850.

limit for Bank of France advances had been reached. These banks were given short-term Treasury securities which, the government secretly promised, could be discounted at the Bank of France. In other words, a new issue of paper money resulting from this type of loan would appear on the statement of the Bank of France not as an increase in Bank-to-Treasury advances, but as an increase in " commercial portfolio." Herriot, faced by impossible deficits and unwilling to precipitate a " crise de confiance " by asking for an increase in Bank advances and notes in circulation, had avoided the previous roundabout method by simply asking the Bank to understate the quantity of notes in circulation.[5] The governor of the Bank of France, Robineau, had brought the issue to a head by threatening to show the Treasury " bankrupt " in the Bank's weekly statement, unless Herriot obtained an increase in the *plafond* from the legislature.[6]

For the next year a long procession of *Cartel* governments—with a total of seven finance ministers [7] and a flock of proposals for financial reform—trooped across the shaky political stage. " One minister scarcely had time to install himself . . . before the desk was cleared for his successor." [8] Bitter debates in the Chamber of Deputies revolved about the conservatives' plan to balance the budget by indirect taxation and the radicals' insistence on direct, heavily progressive taxes. The Left proposals were damned by the Right as " confiscation," and since neither side had a clear-cut majority the controversy was as unproductive as it was acrimonious. It was comparatively easy for various governments to induce the legislature to vote increases in the maximum level of note circulation and Bank of France

5 Haig, *op. cit.*, pp. 118, 213. The actual amount of understatement is unknown; it was probably between .12 and 1.12 billion francs; *La France économique en 1925*, p. 307.

6 Dulles, *op. cit.*, p. 240.

7 MM. Clémentel, de Monzie, Caillaux, Painlevé, Georges Bonnet, Loucheur, and Doumer.

8 Dulles, *op. cit.*, p. 352.

loans, but tax measures proposed at the same time for the eventual reduction of the national debt were invariably voted down.

To meet the heavy amount of bonds which fell due in 1925 the Treasury floated a 4 per cent *rente* which had attractive guarantees against exchange depreciation. The Treasury appealed to the public to redeem its *bons* and two-year Treasury bonds by purchasing these new *rentes*. But this issue only strained the already overloaded money-market. It was put on the market July 20, 1925, and although the sale was to have ended on September 5, the results were so unsatisfactory that the closing date was put off three times, until October 20. Total receipts for the issue were six billion francs instead of the sixteen or eighteen billions expected.[9]

Of all the proposals to ease the pressure on the Treasury, ranging from a higher scale of prices for the government's tobacco monopoly to an outright capital levy, two were given an exceptional amount of attention. The first was based on the theory of the " plafond unique," really a scheme to raise the legal ceiling of notes in circulation. The money-market was so apprehensive at this time that any additional " crashing through the ceiling " might have led to a panic. In view of this situation, Caillaux proposed that the Bank of France be empowered to print additional bank-notes equal to the value of *bons de la défense nationale* outstanding. His argument was based on the supposed fact that these *bons* were circulating virtually as easily as currency;[10] this, he thought, made it possible to establish a " single ceiling " (*plafond unique*) equal to the value of *both* notes and *bons*. The other proposal, by Clémentel, was that the government call in and re-issue all bank-notes, thereby forcing hoarders to bring their money out of hiding or forfeit it, and giving the Treasury the difference be-

9 *La France économique en 1925*, p. 338.

10 See Dulles, *op. cit.*, pp. 247-248, for a personal experience apparently proving that Parisian merchants had entirely different ideas on the " moneyness " of *bons*.

tween the amount of notes officially outstanding and the amount actually turned in for new notes.[11]

These two rather desperate proposals indicate the extent to which panic was dominating the financial scene. By the end of 1925 the seemingly uncontrollable wave of exchange depreciation had brought a hysterical note into many of the contemporary pronouncements on financial affairs. There was a considerable amount of ranting at the inaction of the various governments in the face of the crisis, and economists groaned over the announcement of a prospective Treasury deficit of eleven billion francs for the year 1925.[12] Many writers called for a return to the good old days of the gold standard. Charles Rist, then professor of economics at the University of Paris, insisted that:

> It is necessary to discard all financial romanticism—*ancien régime* as well as revolutionary—and to return once more to the old proved methods which, begun in seventeenth century Holland and continued by England in the eighteenth century, have built the strength and independence of all countries. . . .[13]

Most of the blame was aimed at the Chamber of Deputies because of the deputies' ". . . tendency to deliver themselves up to theoretical discussions, to argue, to split up into factions, to quarrel . . ." [14] During the course of an exhausting session lasting, with a few interruptions, from 4 p.m. December 2 until noon the next day, one of the several Briand governments begged the Chamber to authorize another " extraordinary " advance from the Bank in order to meet the year-end obligations of the Treasury. With despairing logic Briand asked the Cham-

11 *JO, Sénat, Débats*, 1925, p. 532. This tactic was used by several European governments after World War II.

12 *La France économique en 1925*, p. 253. Many years later, the Ministry of Finance reported that the actual budgetary deficit for 1925 was quite small: only 1.5 billion francs. *Inventaire, op. cit.*, p. 230.

13 *La France économique en 1925*, p. 184.

14 *Ibid.*, p. 236.

ber how, if they refused his government the necessary funds, they would solve the problem in any different manner with another government. In the various proposals and counter-proposals made, his government, though it had just been formed, sometimes received a majority of as few as two votes.[15]

The " flight from the franc."—When the feeling of panic finally seeped into the consciousness of the ordinary citizen, the monetary situation in France took a much more serious turn. Faced by the prospect of having his income and his savings turned into worthless paper, remembering the frightening example of the complete collapse of the German currency in 1923, the man on the street joined the men in the Bourse. Together they turned money and monetary securities into goods as fast as possible and tried desperately to buy up foreign securities and to place deposits in foreign banks. Thus was the " flight from the franc " begun.

> Whereas, from 1914 to 1919 the financial problems which had to do with the value of the franc were left in the hands of those professionally equipped to handle such affairs, in 1925 and 1926 every groceryman was considering the effect of the exchange rate on coffee, every stenographer was trying to build up a savings account in a gold standard country. . . . The cost of the dollar was the subject of conversation in every corner café, and one could hardly make a purchase without some discussion of the exchange rate. There was, in fact, a general increase in money consciousness, which made the situation peculiarly hard for the government to handle, and this growing feeling of uncertainty as to the future of all kinds of wealth and on the part of all classes of people led eventually to the hysteria of July, 1926.[16]

The financial sections of the daily papers, heretofore the concern of " hommes d'affaires," now were breathlessly scrutinized

15 *JO, Chambre, Débats*, 1925, pp. 3928-3970.
16 Dulles, *op. cit.*, pp. 45-46.

by all. The Bank of France statement on note circulation was considered especially important: ". . . this one item . . . was capable of precipitating a panic." [17]

The most sought-after haven for those in " flight from the franc " was, of course, gold, but almost equally acceptable were dollars, pounds, and stocks like Suez Canal, Rio Tinto, de Beers, and Royal Dutch, which were pegged to gold and therefore not sensitive to fluctuations in the exchange rates. Some stocks were smuggled into the country to avoid exchange regulations and were sold from hand to hand, outside of the market.[18] Insurance companies, credit societies, cooperatives—all who had invested in *bons de la défense nationale*—were reluctant to renew them in the face of the rapidly dropping purchasing power of the franc. Salaried *fonctionnaires* who were already living close to the margin were forced to draw on their hoards of *bons* to meet living expenses.

The value of *bons* outstanding fell off from 55 to 46 billion francs during the course of 1925, and there was a decided shift toward the very short-term issues of one and three months maturity, and a corresponding drop in the relative amounts of six months and one year *bons*. In general the money-market was characterized by an overabundance of money seeking stocks and short-term bonds and a sharp drop in the demand for investment in long-term government and industrial bonds. The " flight from the franc " was accompanied by a rapidly increasing rate of the turnover of money, one of the chief characteristics of hyper-inflation, in which the disproportionate demand for goods and for " safe " securities merely aggravates the inflationary spiral.

The seriousness of the monetary situation was so evident that in December, 1925 a group of textile manufacturers in the North offered to raise a three billion franc loan to help the Treasury. This unprecedented generosity was refused on the

17 *Ibid.*, p. 46.

18 Bouton, *op. cit.*, p. 127.

ground that it would give too much power to one class and to one section of the country.[19]

During this financial crisis the government made few serious attempts to block the franc's continued fall on the exchange. It enacted a series of regulations enforcing a wartime law of April 3, 1918 forbidding citizens to build up foreign deposits without government permission or to ship out any sort of funds or securities with the purpose of making speculative profits. In July, 1926 the Bank of France was prevailed on to raise its discount rate to the unheard-of height of 7.5 per cent.[20] These feeble measures " affected the ways and means of speculation but not the incentive." Aside from the illegal but common transfer of short-term capital to foreign banks, a legal loophole was exploited by export merchants who left the proceeds of their sales abroad in foreign currency deposited in foreign banks and then sold the ownership of these deposits to speculators. Another easy way to avoid the anti-speculative laws was to conduct business in terms of " sliding-scale " and gold-equivalent contracts, protecting the contractors from losses due to changes in the exchange rates. Some French courts further confused the issue by upholding the legality of these contracts.

The " Committee of Experts."—On May 31, 1926 the desperate government authorized the creation of a " Committee of Experts " who were to investigate the crisis and recommend some feasible way out of the inflationary spiral. Chosen as members of this committee, not without opposition from the Left,[21] were some of the most famous and respected financial leaders from both the business and the academic world.[22] Its

19 Dulles, *op. cit.*, p. 360.

20 L'Institut scientifique de Recherches économiques et sociales, *L'Evolution de l'économie française, 1910-1937, Tableaux statistiques* (Paris: Recueil Sirey, 1937), Table 45.

21 See the speech by Vincent Auriol, May 27, 1926, *JO, Chambre, Débats,* p. 2241.

22 Professors Rist and Jèze, six representatives of powerful banks and investment houses (Lewandowski of the Comptoir National d'Escompte,

report, disclaiming "political preoccupation and doctrinaire preference" and heralded by a great fanfare in the press, appeared on the third of July.[23] Dashing to earth the hopes of the *rentiers,* it recommended the abandonment of any attempt, at least in the near future, to revalorize the franc at its pre-war parity. The "experts" also advocated the substitution of a definite per cent of gold reserves against notes in circulation for the "plafond" system of a legally-authorized maximum. In an important section of their report, the "experts" argued that the troublesome short-term *bons* should be removed from the control of the Treasury and made the responsibility of an independent bureau. A return to the gold standard at a new par, they claimed, should be accomplished as soon as possible, but it would have to await the following conditions: (1) a balanced budget; (2) accumulation of a sufficient amount of gold and foreign exchange for a reserve in the Bank of France; (3) an "adjustment" of the external "political" debt; (4) a normal balance of payments; and (5) "adaptation of economic factors to the new monetary situation"—in other words, a period of comparative calm in the financial world. Meanwhile, immediate steps should be taken to cut fiscal expenditures and to increase indirect taxation.[24]

The tone of the committee's report, urging prompt and drastic action, encouraged Caillaux, Minister of Finance, to ask for decree-making powers to deal with the crisis. This move was defeated when Herriot stepped down from his chair as president of the Chamber of Deputies, delivered a brilliant and im-

---

Masson of the Crédit Lyonnais, Moreau of the Banque d'Algérie, Oudot of the Banque de Paris et de Pays-Bas, Philippe of Lazard Frères, and Simon of the Société Générale), three officials of large industrial associations (Duchemin of the C.G.P.F., Fougère of the Association Nationale d'Expansion Economique, and de Peyerimhoff of the Comité Central des Houillères) and Sergent and Picard of the Bank of France.

23 *Rapport du Comité des Experts* (Paris: Imprimerie Nationale, 1926).

24 Many of these recommendations of the Committee of Experts were eventually adopted by the Poincaré government of 1926.

passioned lecture on the dangers of dictatorship, and succeeded in overthrowing the Briand-Caillaux government. This was the signal for the beginning of the last and most serious phase of the financial panic. Almost anybody who succeeded in placing an order for " forward " pounds or dollars was now assured of a fantastic profit; the atmosphere of panic began to have dangerous resemblances to the recent monetary collapse in Germany, as middle-class families rushed to turn their savings into jewelry, real estate, automobiles, and furniture.[25]

The wealthier financial interests had sold the franc down the river in 1924. It had taken one more year for small investors, and the bulk of the French people, to realize that the attainment of pre-war parity for the franc was a hopeless dream. The " flight from the franc " was an example of the self-frustrating responses which follow a community's sudden mass comprehension of the consequences of a depreciating currency.

Establishment of stability—the Poincaré administration.— When the deputies came out of the Palais Bourbon on July 17, they were faced by an angry, yelling mob. The " little people " were demanding action on the part of their legislature to deal with the financial crisis. A week later the last *Cartel des Gauches* government was formed, once more under Herriot; this government lasted only forty-eight hours, during which the franc fell to 2.0 cents.[26] The Radical-Socialist party, with the balance of power in the Chamber, decided to desert the *Cartel*. On July 25 Poincaré was asked to form a " National Unity " government, and while he chose ministers from the leaders of almost every party, the most important positions were given to conservatives and moderates.

25 Lachapelle, *op. cit.*, p. 138.

26 The new governor of the Bank of France, Emile Moreau, hastened the downfall of the Herriot ministry with much the same threat to disclose the Treasury's " bankruptcy " as that which had been levelled by the previous governor against the Herriot administration in April, 1925. See William A. Brown, Jr., *The International Gold Standard Reinterpreted, 1919-1934* (New York: National Bureau of Economic Research, Inc., 1940), pp. 441-444.

Miraculously the picture seemed to change overnight. The presence of Raymond Poincaré at the head of the government apparently was enough to stop the panic. The character of the man himself and his long record of service to France had a great deal to do with this reversal toward confidence. Essentially austere and undemonstrative, he was recognized by most parties as unimpeachably honest and efficient, exactly the sort of cool head France needed in this moment of despair. " The *Rentiers* of the Right could entrust him with their purses, and the Puritans of the Left could entrust him with their principles." [27] Significantly enough, he kept the finance portfolio for himself.

When the new premier mounted the tribune to deliver his first speech to the Chamber of Deputies, Marcel Cachin yelled out, " We see you only in bad times! " and to show their determined opposition to the new government, he and the other Communist deputies rose and sang the *Internationale.* Through the traditional heckling of other parties in the Chamber, however, one could see an evident conviction that it was now or never—Poincaré the " strong man " or " national bankruptcy." Poincaré assured them that firmness and support for his government would pull France back from the abyss; [28] and after July the unremitting wrangling over fiscal and monetary policy stopped abruptly. The Assembly admitted its incompetence by granting Poincaré power to issue decrees having the force of law on all subjects necessary for the safety of the franc.

The new premier proceeded to use his powerful position with extreme caution. He made no frontal attack on the problems of the national debt or the exchange rate, hoping rather that they would resolve themselves if only confidence could be restored. In a gesture to the industrialists, therefore, the supertax on the highest income brackets was reduced from 60 to 30 per cent. The business turnover tax of 1920 (2 per cent *chiffre*

27 Peel, *The Economic Policy of France*, p. 136.

28 *JO, Chambre, Débats*, 1926, p. 3036.

d'affaires) was made to apply to every conceivable business transaction, and it soon proved to be a lucrative source of revenue.[29] The luxury tax was raised to 12 per cent, and import duties were slightly increased. All these were measures designed to improve old rather than to create new taxes, and all were in line with the conservatives' contention that the Treasury should be supported by indirect taxes which were paid by all taxpayers, rather than by "confiscatory" taxes paid only by the wealthy.

The Caisse d'amortissement.—The next important financial measure of the new government was given the dignity of a constitutional amendment by a joint session of the Chamber of Deputies and the Senate at Versailles on August 10, 1926. There the members of the National Assembly solemnly authorized the establishment of a new institution with the grand title of *La Caisse autonome de gestion des bons de la défense nationale, d'exploitation industrielle des tabacs, et d'amortissement de la dette publique,* commonly (and hopefully) shortened to the *Caisse d'amortissement.* By the terms of this constitutional amendment the *Caisse d'amortissement* was to be responsible to the Ministry of Finance and would act in support of the Treasury while remaining "autonomous." Its director was to be nominated by the minister of finance and appointed by the President of the Republic, and its executive commission was to include highly-placed and capable economic and financial experts. Its main job was to take charge of the burdensome "floating" debt—the short-term Treasury bonds and the *bons de la défense nationale.* Its funds were provided by the revenues from the government's tobacco monopoly, the tax on the first transfer of real estate, and inheritance duties.

This demonstration on the part of the government, sometimes sneeringly referred to as "le geste de Versailles," was frankly intended to build up the all-important element of public

29 Income from the *chiffre d'affaires* tax rose from 2.5 billion francs in 1925 to 6.5 billions in 1926 and to 7.5 billions in 1927. *Le Temps,* Jan. 7, 1929.

confidence in the new government's firm attitude toward financial matters. The rather meaningless insistence on the " autonomy " of the *Caisse d'amortissement* was a deliberate attempt to circumvent the deep-seated French distrust in the ability of bureaucrats successfully to manage monetary affairs.

To the confusion of the skeptics, the *Caisse d'amortissement* began to show good results almost immediately: it resolved the problem of the very short-term *bons* which had proved a constant source of embarrassment to the Treasury. These *bons* had maturity dates of one month, three months, six months, and one year; every panic had brought them in a flood to the Treasury. This meant that the Treasury had been forced to pay out large amounts of cash just when it might least have been able to do so. The director of the *Caisse d'amortissement* now simply allowed each of the various short-term *bons* to pass out of existence as soon as there was money enough to redeem the issue falling due. Thus the one-month *bons* disappeared from the market December 16, 1926; the three-month issues were discontinued January 16, 1927; the six-month *bons* suffered a similar fate later in the same month. By June, 1927 the *Caisse d'amortissement* was in such a strong position that it began to reduce the number of one-year *bons*. The success of this institution entrenched it so firmly in the affections of French financiers and economists that there was some talk of the advisability of entrusting it with the management of the long-term as well as the " floating " debt.[30]

The " de facto stabilization " of the franc.—While the *Caisse d'amortissement* was contributing so satisfactorily to the " assainissement " of the financial situation, Poincaré was beginning the complicated task of stabilizing the exchange rate of the franc. As soon as he had taken office, increased confidence had manifested itself in a slackening demand for foreign exchange, and the franc began to show more strength on the Bourse. Nominally the franc was still established at the pre-war

30 *La France économique en 1928*, p. 418. The *Caisse d'amortissement* is still (1950) one of the important French financial institutions.

" Germinal " par of 19.31 cents and 322 milligrams of gold, although since August 5, 1914 France had been off the gold standard and the franc had fallen steadily in relation to other currencies and to gold.

Now the government announced that it would establish a " de facto stabilization." [31] In other words, the franc would be restrained from fluctuating on the exchange, although no legal par value would be set against gold or foreign currencies. Later, when prices achieved some sort of equilibrium and the Treasury and the Bank of France deemed the situation favorable, the franc would be placed on a new and permanent basis. The first important step in this direction was a law of August 7, 1926, by which the Assembly ratified a number of " conventions " which Poincaré had had drawn up between the Treasury and the Bank of France. By the terms of this law:

(1) The law forbidding the Bank of France to buy foreign bills of exchange (February 12, 1916) was revoked.

(2) The Bank was authorized to buy gold and currency on the open market.

(3) The minister of finance was authorized to draw up agreements with the Bank of France regarding Treasury loans and the limit of note circulation.

(4) Notes printed by the Bank against its newly acquired reserves were not to be counted against the " plafond " established July 22, 1926.

The provision of the law of August 7, 1926 giving the Bank of France the right to engage in buying and selling of bills of exchange proved highly successful. The Bank simply bought francs when its directors believed the exchange rate was too low and sold when the opposite was the case. On December 22, 1926 the Bank's representative on the Bourse announced that he would keep the franc at 122.25 per pound sterling; the de facto stabilization of the franc was accomplished. In terms of

31 The Rapport du Comité des Experts had recommended this prestabilization period; op. cit., p. 50.

American currency, the franc had appreciated from two to four cents since the panic month of July, 1926.

Large amounts of foreign currencies were offered to the Bank of France, now that the "men on the inside" believed that the franc was due for a rise. The Bank rapidly turned a large quantity of these foreign notes into gold by presenting them at the various central banks for payment. So much of the Bank of England's gold reserve was depleted in this manner that financial interests in England were seriously worried. After repeated representations by Montague Norman, head of the Bank of England, this policy of the French Bank was discontinued.[32]

The triumph of Poincaré.—On February 3, 1928 Raymond Poincaré stood up in the Chamber of Deputies to answer interpellations which had been directed against him, as minister of finance, for the past eight days. It must have been one of the supreme moments of the old man's career. A great number of Frenchmen considered him the man who had saved his country's economic life from utter collapse after so many others had failed, and it is possible that he shared this opinion. Now, with France evidently well on the way to prosperity and the franc on an even keel, he had an opportunity to crush those who still caviled at him and to ridicule those who had opposed his financial measures back in 1926.

Poincaré began this famous speech by stating that he was not going to justify himself or his policies. Let us stick to the facts! he said. The facts, according to Poincaré, were that on the day his government took office the Treasury had exactly one million francs on deposit at the Bank of France. Now the Treasury had a bank balance of 6.5 billion francs. *Violà.* ("Vifs applaudissements au centre et à droite.")

Léon Blum and his friend Vincent Auriol, "Docteur Tantpis," continued Poincaré, had insisted that increased taxes and a higher exchange rate of the franc would drive all the money

32 René Sédillot, *Histoire du franc* (Paris: Recueil Sirey, 1939), p. 327.

out of France. The " Committee of Experts " and others had foretold the ruination of the country if a legal stabilization of the franc was not carried out soon after 1926. Neither prophecy had been borne out by the facts!

All through the session of February 3 and for half of the next day, Poincaré was completely master of the situation. Hecklers on the Left were sarcastically put in their places or freezingly ignored. Long lists of statistical " facts " were read off to prove that " les petits " had benefited from the acts of the Poincaré government as much as had the upper bourgeoisie by the return to financial stability. Poincaré pointed to the great number of increased government pensions, the retirement of nine billion francs of the public debt, decreased tax rates, higher salaries for *fonctionnaires,* and completion of the reconstruction of the war-devastated *départements* as evidence of the wisdom of his policies.

Next Poincaré gave his reasons for the continued postponement of the " *de jure* stabilization " (devaluation). Establishing a new par for the franc is a delicate thing, he said; it requires a return to the gold standard and a bigger gold reserve. France must return to convertibility into gold under conditions which will permit the minimum of injustices and damage to the community.

As to the *rentiers,* said Poincaré, the best solution would evidently be to repay them in full,[33] but now we are faced with the necessity for making the most of a bad situation. The *rentiers* will have to find their consolation in the new stability and prosperity of France and in the higher prices of French *rentes.*[34]

33 This statement created a sensation on the floor of the Chamber. It was several minutes before Poincaré was able to proceed with his speech. See Raymond Poincaré, *La Restauration financière de la France* (Paris: Payot, 1928), p. 105. (A transcript of this speech.)

34 The 3 per cent perpetual *rente* rose from 47.20 francs at the end of June, 1926 to 57.35 francs one year later and to 71.45 francs at the end of June, 1928. National Bureau of Economic Research, file No. 11,21 (unpublished). (Hereinafter referred to as " NBER," with the appropriate file number.)

When Poincaré finished, his supporters in the Chamber swarmed around him to congratulate him on his triumph. His speech was widely circulated in book form; it was eagerly and thoroughly discussed throughout the country and played an important part in the national elections of April, 1928.

The " Poincaré franc."—By the beginning of 1927 it had been evident that the crisis was stopped short of total monetary disaster and that France would not have to go down the road to " national bankruptcy " recently traveled by so many Continental countries. Financial experts had greeted this " return to normalcy " with a chorus of relief and had expressed satisfaction that France was experiencing a " rebirth of the taste for saving "; there was even some back-slapping and pointing with pride:

> Nations which have the firm will to resolve financial and monetary problems by processes which are the lessons of experience are always able to avoid the crises which many countries in Europe are still suffering; our country has been able to deal with that problem, a little too tardily perhaps, but with a courage which does her honor.[35]

Not much ink was spilled over the severe losses sustained by the *rentiers* and the petty bourgeoisie in general; there was too much interest in the return of " normal " financial conditions.

By the end of 1927 bull speculation was creating such a demand for francs that the Bank of France was hard pressed to keep the exchange rate stable. Exporters and those interested in the tourist trade feared a decline in business if the exchange value of the franc should continue to increase; these groups, along with most economists, industrialists, and bankers, began to put pressure on the government to act quickly. They argued that a further appreciation of the franc would have serious depressive effects on the economy.[36] On May 31, 1928 the gov-

---

[35] *La France économique en 1927*, p. 460.

[36] Business cycle statistics for this period actually do show a trough in June, 1927. See Arthur F. Burns and Wesley C. Mitchell, *Measuring Busi-*

ernor of the Bank of France threatened to resign if legal stabilization were not undertaken by the fifteenth of July.[37]

Poincaré himself was reluctant to make a definitive break with the old *Germinal* franc. He hesitated to destroy the last hopes of the *rentiers* that the full value of their savings would be regained, and continued to look for the miracle that would restore the franc to pre-war parity.[38] The *rentier* class, as a whole, had, in fact, suffered a tremendous loss. In 1913 there had been 31.2 billion francs in *rentes* outstanding; by 1926 the cost of living had increased by about 400 per cent, so that approximately 80 per cent of the purchasing power of this investment hinged on the question of revalorization. An additional 100 billion francs in *rentes* had been bought between 1914 and 1921;[39] the *rentiers* stood to lose heavily on these as well. But since the cost of living in France had begun to rise at the start of the war, the heaviest proportional loss was that on the 3 per cent " perpetuals " issued before 1913.

On June 21, 1928, the day when the government finally announced its plans for " *de jure* stabilization," Poincaré let it be known that it was against his own personal wishes: " The ideal thing would assuredly be to be able to proceed with complete revalorization. Besides being a political and moral satisfaction for the whole nation, it would be an act of gratitude toward those who have had confidence in the State. . . ."[40] But, Poincaré concluded, he was convinced that a movement in this direction would precipitate a deflation and a resultant depression;

---

ness Cycles (New York: National Bureau of Economic Research, 1946), p. 78. But this was a relatively slight recession. The number of bankruptcies in 1927, for example, was about the same as in 1926. See *La France économique en 1927*, p. 530.

37 Sédillot, *op. cit.*, p. 331.

38 Robert Wolff, *Economie et finances de la France, passé et avenir* (New York: Brentano's, 1943), p. 167.

39 *Inventaire*, p. 537.

40 *JO, Chambre, Débats*, 1928, pp. 1998-1999.

the nation would suffer more harm from these than from a devaluation.

On Saturday, June 23, after the Bourse had closed, the Chamber began to debate the government's proposal; it was voted on Sunday and became law Monday, June 25, 1928. By this law, the *Germinal* franc was officially abandoned and the new Poincaré franc was introduced to the world.

This important law reëstablished the franc on the gold standard [41] by declaring that the government would surrender 65.5 milligrams of gold nine-tenths fine per paper franc presented for redemption at the Bank of France.[42] The law which had released the Bank from its obligation to redeem its notes in gold (August 15, 1914) was abrogated, and " gold bullion convertibility " was instituted. Although the Bank was not obliged to redeem small amounts of notes in gold, it was required to surrender gold bullion bars, each weighing about twelve kilograms, for 215,000 francs.[43]

Other sections of the law of June 25, 1928 provided for: revaluation at the new rate of the Bank of France's gold reserves and the Treasury's hoard of demonetized metal (mostly old silver *écus*) ; transferring to the credit of the Treasury all of the Bank's windfall profits due to the revaluations (a matter of about seventeen billion francs) ; transferring to the books of the *Caisse d'amortissement* the wartime Russian debt which

41 The "*Germinal*" standard really had been a "limping bimetallic standard," with silver used for some coins (*écus*), without free minting privileges, but with legal tender power. Between the "*de facto*" and the "*de jure*" stabilizations France really had a "gold exchange standard," since the franc was pegged to the pound sterling, at that time a gold standard currency.

42 The old *Germinal* franc had been exchangeable for about 322 milligrams of gold.

43 It is usually assumed that a "true" gold standard (or specie gold standard) involves redeeming notes of a small enough value to allow gold coins to circulate freely. Following the example of England, France avoided the "waste" of internal gold circulation but provided the means whereby gold could settle international accounts. See Pirou, *Cours*, pp. 452-454.

the Soviet government had refused to honor (about 5.9 billion francs); and substituting for the old "plafond" a minimum gold reserve of 35 per cent against total sight obligations —that is, demand deposits and notes in circulation.[44]

The "extraordinary" loans of the State from the Bank of France had been reduced by the Poincaré administration to about fifteen billion francs by this time; the revaluation of the Bank's gold reserves now gave the Treasury a net credit of two billion francs on the books of the Bank of France. The only "passif" remaining was the total of 3.2 billion francs in "permanent loans" which the State had received from the Bank since the latter's establishment, in return for granting renewals of its charter.

THE FRENCH ECONOMY IN THE POST-WAR DECADE

The records of French trade and industry during these years give us a strangely different impression from that received in the agitated domain of fiscal and monetary history. The French world of business seemed to thrive even while the franc was foundering. In terms of production and employment the years 1922–1926 were relatively prosperous for France, despite the financial panics.[45] The sharp rise in prices provided a stimulus to general business activity. Even the depreciation of the franc was not an unqualified disaster; since it proceeded at a faster rate than the rise in the costs of production in France, it made French goods and services relatively cheap and tended to provide a favorable balance of current payments.

Industrial production.—After the 1920–1921 depression, industrial production in France made a tremendous recovery from an index of 49 in October, 1921 to 117 in October, 1924.[46] Apart from the stimulus of profits to be made from ris-

44 For the full text of this law see Haig, *op. cit.*, pp. 438-442.

45 W. Ogburn and W. Jaffe, *The Economic Development of Post-War France* (New York: Columbia University Press, 1929), p. 67.

46 *SGF*, 1913 = 100.

CHART 1. THE EXCHANGE RATE OF THE FRANC AND INDUSTRIAL
PRODUCTION IN FRANCE, 1919–1928

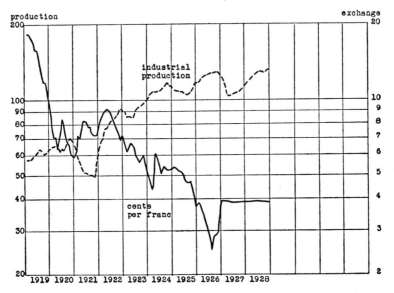

SOURCES: Industrial Production, *SGF*, Index of Industrial Production,
1913 = 100. Exchange rates, *Federal Reserve Bulletin.*

ing prices, industrial output was expanded to meet the need
for rebuilding the war-devastated regions of France.[47] During
the first half of 1925 the level of French industrial production,
in sympathy with the world cyclical recession, slipped from an
index of 113 to 105, in spite of the fact that prices were rising
rapidly in response to the sharp inflationary developments
within France. During the first half of 1926 the index of industrial production rose again to 126, only to level out and
fall back to 105 during the recession which accompanied the
de facto stabilization of the franc in December. In June, 1927
industrial production began a steady climb which did not end
until June, 1930, at an index of 144, the highest level of output
attained between the two World Wars.

47 Ogburn and Jaffe, *op. cit.*, pp. 180-181.

Income and employment.—According to the estimates of L. Dugé de Bernonville, French national income during these years rose steadily from 36 billion francs in 1913 to 227 billions in 1928. By 1923 national income had risen to 134 billions, a rise of about 270 per cent over 1913; the index of the cost of living [48] rose about 350 per cent during the same period; this seems to indicate a considerable loss in the purchasing power of the average citizen's income. But from 1923 until 1928 the index of the cost of living rose from 345 to 531, or about 54 per cent, much less than the 70 per cent increase in the nominal value of the national income, indicating a considerable gain in " real " national income during these years.[49]

TABLE 3

WAGES AND COST OF LIVING, 1922–1928 *

	1922	1923	1924	1925	1926	1927	1928
Average Hourly Wages 22 Skilled Trades (Yearly Average; 1911 = 100)	...	...	440	472	580	582	597
Average Daily Wage of Miners (Last Quarter; in francs)	17.06	21.32	22.87	24.11	32.02	30.69	31.49
Cost of Living in Paris (Last Quarter; 1914 = 100)	300	345	377	421	545	498	531

* Sources: Hourly wages, *Annuaire Statistique;* Miners' wages and cost of living, *SGF.*

The fall in the purchasing power of the franc did not affect the relative position of the industrial proletariat as seriously as it did that of the lower middle classes, since most workers were

48 *SGF*, working-class family of four in Paris, 1914 = 100.

49 Dugé de Bernonville himself, in view of the unreliability of his national income estimates (which tend to be underestimations because they are based on income tax returns) refuses to divide his figures by the cost of living or any other index. See *La France économique en 1936*, pp. 549-550. Froment and Gavanier have estimated a 96 per cent increase in national income from 1923 to 1928. See Appendix II.

not so concerned with the decreasing value of savings and *rentes*. Workers' salaries during and after the war had been increased enough so that in 1925 their real wages were only slightly lower than in 1914.[50] This was partly due to the irregular movement of prices during the inflation. The price of bread, for instance, was held down by good wheat crops; increases in rents had been restricted by governmental order since the war; the cost of many governmental services did not rise at all.

As far as can be determined by the scanty information at our disposal, the recession which was begun by the stabilizing activities of the Poincaré régime affected employment only slightly. The number of unemployed on public relief rolls rose from 17,000 in December, 1926 to 80,000 in February, 1927, but this still represented only a small fraction of the total occupied population.[51] The minister of labor took steps to reduce unemployment by recommending to employers a policy of " short time " rather than dismissals and by operating the classic " safety valve " represented by immigrant workers in France. During 1927 France admitted 64,325 immigrant workers, mostly for the purpose of harvesting crops; 89,982 foreign workers, on the other hand, had their applications for extension of visa refused. Public employment office representatives insisted that employers fill their needs with local labor as far as possible before requesting admission of foreign help to France.

Balances of payments.—The spectacular monetary events in France had repercussions in the realm of international trade and finance, repercussions which lasted several years after the stabilization of the franc was completed. The immediate postwar years saw French economic relations with the outside world completely disorganized owing to the serious damages

50 *La France économique en 1925*, p. 219.

51 *La France économique en 1927*, p. 977. The figures for unemployment in France at this time are unreliable; the many groups not admitted to public relief rolls are not included, and no provision is made for partial unemployment.

of war and the end of inter-Allied economic and financial co-operation. France had always imported the bulk of her industrial raw materials, and these needs were augmented now by the reconstruction effort. A heavy deficit in the balance of commodity trade in 1919 and 1920 was the result. But the depression of 1920–1921 trimmed some of this excess of imports by lowering general business activity.[52] The trend toward reduced imports was soon to be emphasized by the depreciation of the franc.

At first the depreciation was not accompanied by the heavy flight of capital that marked the years 1924–1926. In the early post-war period many of the short-term capital movements were equilibrating in effect, since capital tended to enter France each time the franc suffered a considerable drop in its exchange value. This paradox is explained by the common misinterpretation of the " purchasing-power-parity " theory at that time. Many speculators reasoned that since the purchasing power of the franc in France was high in relation to its worth in foreign exchange the exchange rate of the franc was bound to rise. In time, of course, it was the price structure of France which adapted itself to the exchange rate, and not vice versa.

By 1924 the speculators had been disillusioned, and the movements of capital turned heavily against France. There is little reliable information on the volume of these flights of capital, but estimates have placed them at between forty and fifty billion Poincaré francs for the years 1924–1926 alone.[53]

52 Apart from the *volume* of imports, in 1921 there was a relatively large drop in the *price* of French imports, which for the most part were raw materials, especially sensitive to the world price decline. This also temporarily relieved the pressure on the exchange rate of the franc.

53 All the figures expressed in francs in this section have been reduced for comparability to the stabilized 1928 Poincaré francs. Since 1945 was the first year in which the French government took official notice of France's balances of payments, these figures are based on the estimates in *La France économique* by Pierre Meynial for the years 1920-1933 and by Léonard Rist and Philippe Schwob for the years 1934-1938. These estimations are also used by the League of Nations trade publications (1920-1929—Economic and

Luckily for the central bank's gold reserves, these capital movements could not involve an outflow of gold, since France was still off the gold standard. A certain amount of relief from pressure on the exchange rates came in 1924 with the beginning of regular reparations payments from Germany.[54]

The franc was an obviously "undervalued" currency by 1924; in other words, it was cheaper in terms of foreign exchange and gold than in French goods and services.[55] This meant that it became more profitable for foreigners to import French goods. Tourists flocked to France rather than to other centers of tourism. On the other hand the French now found foreign goods relatively more expensive. To the extent that depreciation was speeded by the "flight from the franc," the disparity between French and foreign prices was aggravated. Exports increased and imports dwindled; as a result the customary deficit in the French balance of trade was practically wiped out.

Reduced deficits in the balance of commodity trade and high income from tourists, interest, dividends, and other "invisible" exports made for an enormous surplus in the "balance of payments on current account." This current balance, as distinguished from the balance on capital account, is especially important since it enters directly into the flow of national income. In 1924, 1925, and 1926 the annual current surplus averaged over thirteen billion Poincaré francs.

Financial Section, *Memorandum on International Trade and Balances of Payments*; 1930-1938—Economic Intelligence Service, *Balances of Payments*).

54 About three billion Poincaré francs annually from 1924 to 1927; from 1927 to 1930 reparations payments rose from 4.2 to 7.1 billion francs.

55 We are aware of the unanswerable criticisms directed against calculations of the magnitude of under- or overvaluation by "purchasing-power-parity" theorists. Calculations of parities between the United States and France at this time, using 1930 as a base year and cost-of-living indexes, produce some astonishing results. We submit these annual averages of the franc's undervaluation, for what they are worth:

1924—19 per cent	1927—15 per cent
1925—47 per cent	1928—14 per cent
1926—33 per cent	1929— 7 per cent

During these years American tourists alone spent about five billion francs annually in France or about three times as much as in 1913, after taking into account the depreciation of the franc.[56] The rise in the exchange value of the franc during the second half of 1926 cut down the number of tourists in the moderate income groups, but world prosperity after 1927 saw the heyday of the wealthy tourist influx in France. In 1928 the value of the tourist trade in France (7.5 billion francs) by itself more than offset the unfavorable balance of commodity trade (4.5 billion francs).

The depreciation of the franc came to an end in the summer of 1926, and the surpluses in the balances of payments on current account were sharply reduced. But equilibrium in French trade was not yet restored. The *de facto* and *de jure* stabilizations evidently retained a certain element of undervaluation. A considerable current surplus—about nine billion francs—appeared in both 1927 and 1928. There is no evidence that the French government deliberately undervalued the franc in order to retain its country's advantage in foreign trade. The *de facto* stabilization rate of 122.25 francs per pound sterling was chosen by the Bank of France as a temporary expedient. That the *de facto* became the *de jure* rate, it will be recalled, was due to fears on the part of the Bank (and other financial and industrial interests) that bull speculation would drive the exchange rate of the franc up to a dangerously overvalued level. Whatever the motives involved, the franc remained an undervalued currency until 1930, with all the advantages for export that this entailed.

While the Poincaré régime saw few abrupt changes in the French balances on current account, the trend of capital movements was completely reversed after 1926. The influx of capital which followed the *de facto* stabilization might have been expected to result in a great appreciation of the franc. But the new power of the Bank of France to buy foreign exchange (law of August 7, 1926) checked this possibility. We cannot estimate

56 *La France économique en 1926*, pp. 278-279.

precisely how much short-term capital was "mopped up" by these stabilizing purchases, because the weekly statement of the Bank of France disguised such operations by including them in "actifs divers" (sundry assets). After remaining at about four billion francs all through 1926, the "divers" rose precipitously to ten billions by March, 1927 and to twenty-one billions three months later; when the *de jure* stabilization was undertaken (June, 1928) the "divers" stood at thirty-one billion francs.[57] This at least gives a hint that the exchange value of the franc would have risen much higher than four cents (or 65.5 milligrams of gold) if it had been allowed to do so.

The money-market.—During these years of monetary crises the Paris money-market was dominated by changes in the national "floating" debt. For the most part this very short-term debt was made up of the *bons* of from one month to two years maturity, plus the "extraordinary" advances of the Bank of France to the State, both important for their effect on "confidence." The obvious and constantly increasing pressure on the Treasury to ask for more funds at a time when the franc was weakening made investors wary of government securities of more than one year's maturity. By the time of the "flight from the franc," therefore, the national debt was weighted heavily to the side of short-run obligations, which meant that the Treasury was completely at the mercy of investors unwilling to renew their *bons*. By the end of 1924 the *bons* were maturing at the rate of seven or eight billion francs each month.

During 1925 there was a drop from fifty-five billion francs in *bons de la défense nationale* outstanding to forty-six billions. The money-market in general, moreover, was characterized by a relative abundance of capital offered for short-term securities, and the percentage of *bons* of very short duration increased as the financial panic deepened.

57 *L'Evolution de l'économie française*, Table 41.

PERCENTAGE OF *Bons de la défense nationale* OUTSTANDING [58]

	January 1, 1925	December 31, 1925
One month	5 per cent	10.7 per cent
Three months	4.6	7.5
Six months	15.7	8.1
One year	74.7	73.7

During the hysterical legislative debates over financial problems in the first part of 1926 purchases of *bons* ground almost to a halt. Financiers were mortally afraid of radical projects calling for the " consolidation " of the short-term debt, or " debt moratoriums," or even capital levies.

This precarious situation was ended by the Poincaré régime of 1926. With the reappearance of stability in the money-market, the Bank of France lowered its discount rate from 7.5 per cent to 6.5 per cent at the end of 1926, to 5 per cent in April, 1927, and to 3.5 per cent by the beginning of 1928. At the same time, when bull speculation was increasing the amount of available funds in Paris, the national debt was successfully shifted toward the long-run obligations. *Rentes* outstanding between July, 1926 and December, 1928 (other than the 3 per cent " perpetual " *rentes*) rose from 43.6 to 102.2 billion francs, while the " dette moyenne " (two to twenty-five year bonds) was reduced by 23.1 billions and the " dette flottante " by 56.3 billions.

REDUCTIONS IN THE " FLOATING DEBT "
JULY 31, 1926–DECEMBER 31, 1928 [59]

	July 31, 1926	Dec. 28, 1928
Bons du Trésor (controlled by Treasury)	2,963 millions	384 millions
Bons du Trésor and *de la défense nationale* (controlled by the *Caisse d'amortissement*)	44,218	35,665
Extraordinary advances of the Bank of France	37,450	0
Deposits in the Treasury	8,378	671
	93,009	36,720

58 *La France économique en 1925*, p. 303.

59 *La France économique en 1928*, p. 412.

Another important factor in French monetary developments, the advances of the Bank of France to the State, continued to dominate the total supply of currency in circulation, as it had ever since the outbreak of World War I. Changes in currency in circulation were linked almost entirely to changes in the " extraordinary " advances, so that the correlation ratio of these two factors had rarely dropped below + .9 between 1915 and 1927.[60]

CHART 2.   BANK-NOTE CIRCULATION AND BANK-TO-STATE ADVANCES
IN FRANCE, 1919–1928

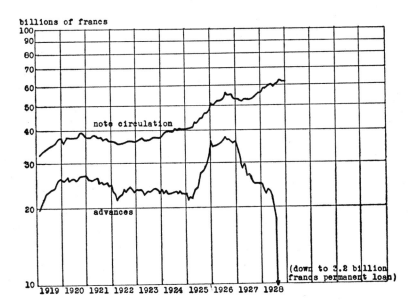

SOURCES : Note circulation, *SGF* ; advances, *Bulletin de Statistique et de législation comparée.*

It should be emphasized, however, that the trend of advances after 1920 was steadily if slightly downward, and that neither advances nor note circulation rose to any great extent until the volume of *bons* outstanding began to fall off. Increases in note

60 Rogers, *op. cit.*, p. 170.

circulation during the First World War had been linked unmistakably to budgetary deficits by the intermediary of Bank
advances. But the inflationary pressure in 1925 was the result
of an entirely different set of circumstances. The budget for
that year, in fact, was practically in balance, and the increase
in the national debt hardly large enough to account for the
sort of bear speculation and financial panic evident in the
" flight from the franc." The key to French fiscal difficulties in
1925 was not to be found in budgetary deficits, but rather in
the increasing pressure from the floating debt.

After 1926 the reverse flow of capital to France and the increase in gold reserves could have been expected to work an
enormous expansion of the volume of currency in France. But
the note circulation of the Bank of France rose by only ten billion francs between the end of 1926 and the end of 1928. The
explanation is simple. The currency released by the Bank's
purchases of gold and foreign exchange during the *de facto* stabilization was partially " neutralized " by the repayment of
thirty-seven billion francs in advances from the Bank. The improved position of the Treasury which allowed this repayment
was due to the improvement of tax receipts in the Poincaré
administration, the resumption of satisfactory purchases of
bons, and, most important of all, the revaluation of the Bank's
gold reserves in the spring of 1928. While the volume of bank-
notes remained relatively stable, the credit structure of the
country was greatly enlarged. One year after the advent of
the Poincaré government, deposits at the Bank of France had
risen from 4.0 to 12.5 billion francs, but thereafter the trend
was downward, reaching 6.5 billion francs at the end of 1928.
At the " Big Four " commercial banks demand deposits rose
from 22.5 billion francs to 34.3 billions during the years 1927–
1928.

*French prices and exchange rates 1919–1928; some theoreti-
cal considerations.*—The monetary developments in France
during the decade after the First World War have received a

formidable amount of attention from specialists in monetary theory. The dramatic spectacle of a formerly stable currency, removed from its gold moorings and fluctuating with hardly any interference from the central bank or the government, stands as a challenge to all who would espouse a general theory of money. It may be worth while to summarize a few of the implications for monetary theory of French exchange rate fluctuations, even though only a sketchy presentation is possible here.

Just after the First World War the most commonly accepted explanation of these developments rested on the " purchasing-power-parity approach," essentially a corollary of the quantity theory of money. According to this view, the currency inflation during the war and after led to a steep rise of prices in France; because of the relative cheapness of foreign goods and services there was an increase in the demands of French importers for foreign exchange and a decrease in the demands of foreigners for francs. Thus currency inflation brought about exchange depreciation *via* an increase in the domestic price structure.

More popular in Germany than in France was the " balance of payments approach," which employed the truism that the price of any article—including foreign exchange—is determined by supply and demand. This approach was used to show that capital flights, reparations transfers, and other factors not necessarily involved in the relative dearness of foreign and domestic goods may bring about a demand for foreign currency and lead to exchange depreciation.

In France, on the other hand, several economists formulated a rather different approach, which they called the " psychological theory of money." [61] They pointed out that the other theories assumed a line of causality either from prices to exchange rates (purchasing-power-parity) or vice versa (pay-

---

[61] The chief proponents of this theory in France were Albert Aftalion and Gaëtan Pirou.

ments). But according to the "psychological theory" at the heights of monetary crises neither prices nor exchange rates was the independent variable; both were under the control of "psychological" expectations of speculators, shopkeepers, *rentiers, etc.*

If these views are considered as complementary, rather than contradictory, they form a fairly good theoretical explanation of the monetary developments during the first few post-war years. Obviously the huge imports of goods into war-devastated France gave that country a heavily unfavorable balance of current payments and led to a sharp depreciation of the franc during 1919. On the other hand, the *magnitude* of the depreciation (the dollar rose about three-fold) corresponds roughly to the increase in French wholesale and retail prices by the end of the war. Whether or not the mechanism described by the purchasing-power-parity theory was operative, the fact that speculators *believed* in this theory led, as we have seen, to an inflow of capital and a temporary halt of exchange depreciation in the spring of 1920.

When the sharp rates of inflation and depreciation were resumed after the depression of 1920-1921, and especially after the dissipation of the "phantom of reparations," several new factors, best explained by the more modern "income approach," came upon the scene.[62] During the "attack on the franc" in 1924, international capital movements at last turned decisively against France. The flight of capital brought about a rapid decline in the franc, which now became an "undervalued" currency. As a result of the relative cheapness of her goods and services, France enjoyed a large surplus in the balance of payments on current account. This acted to boost the already-rising French national income, and sharpened competition for domestic goods. The result was a rise in the price structure

62 This argument follows that in the League of Nations publication, *The Course and Control of Inflation* (Princeton: Princeton University Press, 1946), pp. 49-50.

CHART 3. THE COURSE OF INFLATION IN FRANCE, 1919–1928

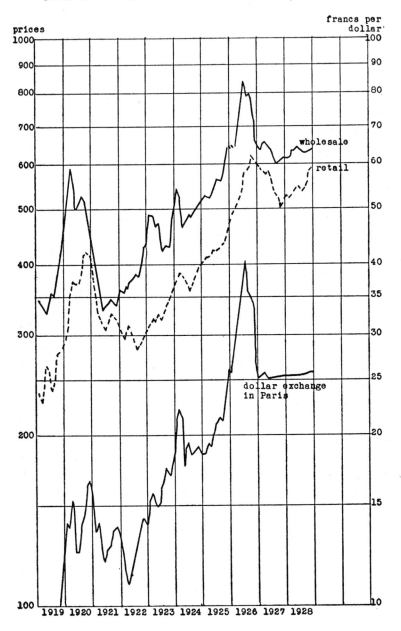

even while business activity slowed down during the slight business recession of 1924-1925.[63]

The tendency for French prices to rise was aggravated by the existence of full employment, or at least by a shortage of the factors of production. It will be recalled that wages were rising more steeply than the cost of living, that unemployment was negligible, and that in fact thousands of foreign workers were being imported. National money income rose much more rapidly than did production, at least between 1923 and 1926; the inevitable result was a severe inflation of French prices. Because of the undervaluation of the currency, furthermore, a large fraction of domestic production was being shipped abroad as the counterpart of the capital flight, which further reduced the volume of goods available to French producers and consumers.

While this explanation seems fairly satisfactory for the years 1923-1924, with the "flight from the franc" in 1925 forces were unleashed which completely by-passed the causal sequence from exchange rates to price inflation *via* changes in income, which we have just described. The capital flight continued to put a downward pressure on the franc. But now an "internal

---

[63] See Charts 1 and 3. This pressure on prices, unlike that during the war, was not linked to budgetary deficits and resultant increases in bank-note circulation. As we have seen above, by 1924 the budgetary deficit was being reduced and in 1925 it was negligible. Currency circulation and advances from the Bank of France were not raised until the "flight from the franc" in 1925. Nor was there a rise in the volume of bank money; bank deposits at the "Big Four" commercial banks and at the Bank of France also remained steady until 1925. In 1925 deposits at the "Big Four" suddenly jumped to twenty billion francs after remaining at fourteen or fifteen billions all during 1923 and 1924; this may reflect the liquidation of *bons* which played such an important part in the "flight from the franc."

CHART 3. (*Opposite page*)
SOURCE: *SGF*. For wholesale prices, the period 1919-1925 is based on the July, 1914 index and is made up of 45 articles. The period 1926-1928 is based on the 1913 index and is made up of 126 articles. For the retail price index the base period is July, 1914, and thirteen articles are included.

flight" appeared, to complicate the situation. The bearish "self-fulfilling prophecy" of exchange speculators was reinforced by pessimistic expectations regarding the future of French prices. Now that money began to lose the function of a store of value in the eyes of the community, there was an "internal flight" in the form of purchases of hoarded gold, jewelry and other valuables, and real estate. The movements of exchange rates and prices now were influenced by a complex demand for *both* foreign currency and "money-commodities" in France.[64]

The confluence of these two forces—the internal and external flights from the currency—produced a simultaneity of exchange depreciation and price inflation not easily explainable in quantitative theoretical terms. During the "general increase of money consciousness" in 1925-1926 shopkeepers and manufacturers simply synchronized their prices with the latest exchange quotations from their daily papers.[65] From the resignation of the Herriot government in April, 1925 to just after the *de facto* stabilization at the end of 1926, the correlation of French wholesale prices and exchange rates was almost perfect.[66] This is true for both nationally-produced and imported goods.[67] The prices of nationally-produced goods followed the

[64] Another "flight from the franc" which took the form of rising demand for foreign currency *and* gold *and* money-commodities (e. g., cigarettes) was apparent in France after 1944. The element which produced a black market in currencies in the years following World War II—exchange control—was matched to some degree in the years 1924-1926 by the inability of the "amateur cambist" to obtain access to the rather exclusive institutions dealing in international finance.

[65] Those who did not soon suffered from rising replacement costs. See League of Nations, *Course and Control of Inflation*, p. 53.

[66] Rogers, *op. cit.*, p. 112. See also Dulles, *op. cit.*, p. 319. On the basis of correlation techniques, Rogers has estimated that at times fluctuations in exchange rates led the price movements of nationally-produced commodities by a month or two. According to the purchasing-power-parity concept, changes in domestic prices must precede changes in exchange rates.

[67] According to the *SGF* indexes of the components of the wholesale price index of forty-five articles. But see the criticism of this index in the section on prices in Chapter III.

prices of imported goods (which, of course, are dependent on exchange fluctuations) more or less erratically until the " attack on the franc "; then both indexes came sharply together. Through all of 1925 they remained highly coordinated, and during the first half of 1926 the movements of both sorts of prices were almost perfectly coordinated, both as to direction and as to magnitude.

It seems clear that during the flight from the franc of 1925-1926 " psychological " factors had a direct and decisive influence on both price and exchange rate movements.[68] Expectations of price rises led people to raise prices; the measuring-stick which they used to decide upon the size of the price boosts was the extent of the depreciation of the franc. The rapidity with which Poincaré produced " assainissement " from imminent collapse in 1926, furthermore, and the ease with which all aspects of the crisis were dissipated, seem to give aid and comfort to the proponents of the " psychological theory."

" Psychological " factors also were responsible for the first serious inflation of the currency since 1920. In 1925, when the *rentiers* began to unload their *bons,* the Treasury was forced to obtain loans from the central bank. This increase in banknotes was poured into the business world, where it speeded up the rising velocity of circulation and aggravated the pressure on French prices.

This " psychological theory " has been criticized on the grounds that it is not a theory at all, but merely an admission by the person advancing it that he regards the phenomena under study as economically incomprehensible. To have an economic bearing the qualitative " psychological " attitudes of men must be translated in some manner into supply and demand relationships of money and goods, which are essentially quanti-

---

68 We do not mean to imply that other factors—increase in the velocity of currency circulation, cyclical expansion, increases in national income through surpluses in the balance of current payments—may be ignored. But while France was thus on the edge of hyper-inflation, these factors seem to have played a secondary role.

tative.[69] This seems to be an eminently reasonable point of view, but it is difficult to conceive how specific measurements could be applied to some of the phenomena which we have described. Whether the phrase used is " psychological phenomena " or " the cumulative movements of prices, exchange rates, and of expectations regarding prices and exchange rates," we can expect that, to some degree, most theoretical expositions must fall back on historical description when referring to French monetary events from 1923 to 1927.

MONETARY POLICY IN THE RECONSTRUCTION DECADE

The student of French monetary policy during the reconstruction period cannot help but wonder at the ineptitude of those entrusted with French financial policy. On the one hand, one hears the anguished cries of economists, politicians, and financiers frightened by inflated prices and the dwindling exchange value of the franc; on the other hand, one is struck by the strange fact that for more than three years hardly any vigorous steps were taken to solve this problem. Why?

It is evident, first of all, that simple ignorance of monetary economics was partly to blame. The body of theory in this field we now possess was elaborated as a result of the monetary experiences of the inter-war decades, and was not available to those struggling with monetary problems just after the First World War. Price inflation on the order of that between 1923 and 1926 was unknown since the French Revolution; a hundred years of monetary stability intervened. The lesson of two severe crises was necessary to drive home the absence of any natural law in the relationship: one dollar equals five francs.

The failure of the franc to be reëstablished on its pre-war gold parity through the automatic workings of monetary law shocked the French, but it did not change their essentially metaphysical outlook on money. If there were some legislators

---

69 Michael A. Heilperin, *International Monetary Economics* (London: Longmans, Green and Co., 1939), p. 112.

who were convinced that correct monetary policy involved taking bold steps to meet unusual or rapidly changing situations, they were certainly in the minority. Most Frenchmen still believed that the proper function of monetary policy was to allow the unhampered play of monetary law. This explains the frustrating indecision of legislative debates on financial matters during these years. The lack of any accepted policy allowed political and class conflicts regarding the burden of war expenditures to complicate the situation. The enemies of the *Cartel des Gauches* were doubtless quite pleased to observe the financial difficulties of the administration in 1924 and 1925. If these difficulties had been attended by economic distress such as France experienced in 1935, the legislature might have been led to agree on a program of action more quickly. But the economic milieu of the reconstruction period did not have the desperate qualities of the depression years; the monetary crises of 1924 and 1926 were artificial in the sense that the " real " French economy was apparently sound.

While in a democracy the legislature can hardly be expected to have a better grasp of monetary matters than does its constituency, we should have thought that France deserved better things of its financial leadership. The strangely neutral position of the Bank of France, for example, is difficult to explain. Until 1926 it was the official policy of the Bank to revalorize the franc by gradual stages. Even after the " bear squeeze " in 1924 proved that vigorous action on the part of the central government might bring the exchange market into line, the Bank limited its interference to the " classic " (and classically useless) maneuver of discount rate manipulation.

The problem of ministerial instability also shares in the prolongation of France's monetary troubles at this time. Given the unstable political character of France in the early 1920's, a drastic step like the abandonment of pre-war parity probably could have been taken only as a measure of last resort. The myth of revalorization died harder even than that of reparations; while it existed the short-lived ministries found it easy to dodge financial responsibility.

After bungling along almost to the brink of disaster, the French suddenly called up a monetary savior. The necessary miracle was produced. It is well in line with the French *mystique* regarding money that the man who performed the devaluation was heart and soul in favor of revalorization. Everybody regretted that the franc was " worth only four sous," but after all—it might have been worse. Disillusioned rather than enlightened, the harassed French fervently hoped that a " normal " (pre-1914) monetary situation would now prevail.

CHAPTER III

"THE STRONGEST CURRENCY IN THE WORLD"

THE DEPRESSION AND THE TREASURY, 1929-1932

THE appearance of the new, devalued Poincaré franc in the spring of 1928 was greeted with expressions of hope and relief. The devaluation was hailed as a definitive settlement of the self-perpetuating cycle of inflation, fiscal difficulties, and financial panics which made the memory of the years 1922 to 1926 so painful. Once again France had "a true currency, as solidly guaranteed as the strongest currency in the world."[1] At last *rentiers* and employees with fixed salaries might be released from deadening fear of the future. "Normalcy," long deferred but finally achieved, could now characterize the French economy.

A few years after getting her monetary house in order France was confronted with the most serious economic crisis of recent history. At first, we shall see, France was to demonstrate a singular immunity to the Great Depression. While financial panic and wholesale bankruptcy made money scarce elsewhere, capital poured into France to produce a unique situation of monetary plenty. In 1930, when most of the industrial world was bogging down, French industry was, for the most part, still operating at 1929 heights. By 1932, unfortunately, France herself was in the grip of a depression which seemed to grow steadily worse while other countries began to recover. And this depression finally swept away the foundations of the new Poincaré franc just as surely as the First World War had proved fatal to its *Germinal* predecessor.

The "plethoric Treasury."—Thanks to the coincidence of financial stability in France and world-wide prosperity after

[1] Banque de France, *Compte rendu des Opérations de la Banque de France pendant l'année 1928* (Paris: Dupont, 1929), p. 3.

73

1927, the affairs of the French Treasury in 1927, 1928, and 1929 were a source of immense satisfaction to all concerned. "From the monetary point of view," reported the financial chronicler of Le Temps, " we do not perceive any cloud on the horizon." [2] In sharpest contrast to the years of fiscal difficulties before 1926, each year now showed a balanced budget, tax returns exceeding the most optimistic predictions, and a public debt becoming not only more manageable but also, incredibly enough, smaller. The main complaint of contemporary financial oracles seemed to be that the legislature was allowing the spectacle of money available in the nation's coffers to destroy its sense of financial responsibility.[3] There were those who viewed the "plethoric Treasury" as a positive harm, since it increased the propensity for legislative spending orgies.[4]

One of the more ambitious plans for disembarrassing the Treasury of its excess funds was a project for the reconstitution of the national stock of capital equipment ("outillage national"). Many legislators were anxious to refurbish ancient or war-damaged equipment of French highways, canals, ports, and public services, and called upon the government to help by supplying easy credit.[5] First debated in the fall of 1929, the project was resolved into a five-year plan which would require eventually about five billion francs of state credit, advanced through a Caisse de crédit aux départements et communes. From the beginning the Ministry of Finance opposed this project, but in vain; there were too many important political considerations involved.[6] Finally a "first section" of 670 million

2 Le Temps financier et économique, Jan. 7, 1929.

3 La France économique en 1929, p. 489. Also Le Temps, June 3, 1929; Aug. 26, 1929; and Oct. 14, 1929.

4 Germain-Martin, Le Problème financier, 1930-1936 (Paris: Domat-Montchrestien, 1936), p. 26.

5 See articles in Le Temps, September 28, 1929; January 6, 1930; and July 14, 1930; also the report of the Conseil national économique, JO, Lois et Décrets, 1930, pp. 195-200.

6 Germain-Martin, op. cit., pp. 41-43.

francs was voted in March, 1931 by the Chamber. The Senate gave its consent only in November, 1931, two years after the first debates on the subject.

Among the new demands made on the Treasury during these years of budgetary affluence was one for a bonus for all veterans of World War I, holders of the *carte du combattant*. As finally drawn up by the legislature in 1930, this allocation was to provide each veteran with a *rente* of 500 francs upon reaching the age of fifty and another of 1,200 francs at the age of fifty-five.[7] Here again, political expediency, in response to propaganda in support of the bonus by veterans' organizations, proved stronger than the rather hesitant attempts of some members of the government to cut down the amount of the bonus or to raise the age limits when benefits would accrue.

The years 1928-1930 also saw increased expenditures for the military and for national defense, an increase in salaries of government employees to offset the recent monetary devaluation, and an increase in the outlays for *oeuvres sociales* and aid for the victims of floods and of other public disasters. Objections by various ministers of finance or of the budget [8] to these increasing claims on the Treasury were easily overridden, of course, so long as the tax returns remained so unprecedentedly high. Total receipts for 1928 exceeded expenditures by almost four billion francs, and in 1929 and the first three months of 1930 a surplus of almost five and one-half billion francs was achieved.[9]

Not all of this available money, by any means, was turned over to the legislature for expenditures " which were not all equally justifiable." [10] A large fraction of the surplus funds was

7 *JO, Lois et Décrets*, 1930, p. 4233.

8 From 1930 to 1933, to emphasize the importance of budgetary equilibrium, the French government experimented with a separate portfolio for the head of the Office of the Budget. See Appendix IV.

9 *Inventaire, op. cit.*, p. 230.

10 *La France économique en 1929*, p. 489.

used to whittle down national indebtedness. Thus from December 31, 1928 to December 31, 1930 the total public debt (exclusive of the "political" foreign debt and the obligations of the *Caisse d'amortissement*) was reduced from 293 billion to 274 billion francs.[11] The Treasury and the *Caisse d'amortissement* worked together most successfully in reducing foreign "commercial" indebtedness by loaning the railroads and steamship lines enough money to repay their foreign creditors.[12] The *Caisse d'amortissement* continued the process of withdrawing all government bonds possible, to the point where after 1929 it became difficult to find more bond-holders willing to surrender their shares.[13] That the ghost of revalorization was not quite laid is shown by complaints that *rentiers* could never expect any recompense for losses from the recent devaluation if the *Caisse d'amortissement* insisted on buying back all bonds outstanding.[14] Some deputies proposed to compensate those who had purchased *rentes* before the stabilization of the franc, in the interests of "morale and the economic and social future of the country." [15]

The French taxpayers, ". . . after having supported so courageously the crushing burden necessitated by the restoration of public finances and the recovery of the franc, [now expected] to receive the fruits of their effort." [16] And in fact both direct and indirect taxes were cut so as to represent savings to taxpayers of close to six billion francs in the fiscal year 1929-1930 and another two billions in 1930-1931.

To round out the financial "redressement" the fiscal year was changed from its former correspondence with the calendar

11 *Ibid.*, p. 496.

12 *La France économique en 1930*, p. 538.

13 *Le Temps*, January 13, 1930.

14 *La France économique en 1930*, p. 542.

15 *JO, Documents Parlementaires, Chambre (Sessions Extraordinaires)*, 1932, p. 975.

16 *Le Temps*, February 25, 1929.

year to the period April 1 to March 31, beginning in 1930. This made the fiscal year 1929-1930 one of fifteen months (January, 1929-March, 1930). This measure was enacted on the grounds that if the National Assembly were provided with a full three months after the year-end holidays in which to consider the budget, there would be an end to the legislative propensity to approve budgets only well into the fiscal year to which they applied.[17]

During these years the volume of governmental expenses continued to increase, lightened only by the savings on servicing the national debt effected by bond retirements. The budgetary affluence of the years 1927 to 1930 made it easy for the French legislature to ignore demands for reduction in the total amount of government spending. The number of governmental employees (national, departmental, and municipal) tended to increase steadily, rising from 745,000 in 1925 to 858,000 in 1932.[18] The budget for the fiscal year 1929-1930, including supplementary credits, amounted to fifty-nine billion francs, which did not seem excessive, since it covered fifteen months. But the expenditures for the twelve months 1930-1931 were fifty-six billions, twelve billion francs more than in the fiscal year 1928.

First signs of serious deficits.—The budgetary situation for the fiscal year 1930-1931, the first since 1924 to end with a substantial deficit, did give rise to some worried speculations about the future. The returns of the tax on Bourse operations and on business turnover (*chiffre d'affaires*), considered good barometers of business confidence, began to decline during 1930.[19] Although total tax receipts were still high compared to previous years, total expenditures were even higher, partly because of supplementary credits voted during the year for dis-

---

17 In the fifty-year period 1885-1935, only sixteen budgets were voted before the beginning of the fiscal year! Trotabas, *op. cit.*, p. 41.

18 Peel, *The Economic Policy of France*, p. 178.

19 *L'Evolution de l'économie française*, Table 16.

aster relief and national defense. Revenue surpluses accumulated from previous years were so large, however, that the Treasury easily met the deficit without resorting to a new loan.

When the final figures for the fiscal year 1931-1932 were in, they showed a deficit of almost six billion francs, in spite of an arrangement whereby responsibility for another quantity of government bonds outstanding was transferred from the Treasury to the "autonomous" *Caisse d'amortissement*. Previous deficits had been charged to spendthrift deputies who kept their eyes on the coming elections. But the deficits for the 1931-1932 budget were at least in part a reflection of a depressed economy. Both direct and indirect taxes fell below expectations by as much as 25 per cent, and the government had to support increased expenditures for unemployment relief and heavy subsidies to hard-pressed industries. Furthermore, many of the new charges borne by the government, which owed their existence to the "disorders caused by the years of budgetary facility "[20] when they were first debated, came into operation just as the depression was coming home to France.

The immediate reaction of the administrators of the government's financial agencies to this first chill breath of depression was to cut expenses and to increase taxes wherever possible. Implicit in almost all the contemporary discussions of this problem was the belief that only by balancing the budget could the government stave off financial panic. The inability of the people to bear heavier taxes during a time of depression was disregarded. Ministers of finance and of the budget like MM. Chéron, Reynaud, Germain-Martin, and Piétri pictured themselves as fighting almost single-handed against the impossible demands of greedy legislators who were apt to drag their country down to financial ruin.[21]

20 *La France économique en 1931*, p. 606.

21 See the debate on the proposed budget for 1930-1931, *JO, Débats, Chambre*, 1930, pp. 684-685; *Le Temps*, March 11, 1929; and Germain-Martin, *op. cit.*, p. 66.

Unfortunately for these champions of the balanced budget, the character of the Fourteenth Legislature was not such that it would support any drastic retrenchment. Of the 612 deputies elected in 1928, only 187 had been chosen by a clear majority on the first ballot. The parties of the Left had polled 4.9 million votes to 4.4 millions for the supporters of Poincaré's " National Union " government, but the uncooperative stand of the Communists on the second ballot had been responsible for the appearance of 117 " mal élus " in the new Chamber, deputies who obviously would not have been chosen if the parties of the Left had been able to stand together.[22] In November, 1928 the congress of the Radical-Socialist party decided to withdraw its support from the coalition government of " National Union " and commanded its members in the government to resign in order to put the party in a better position to work for more liberal policies. The result was a confused and divided legis-lature which chose to let fiscal affairs drift along rather than jeopardize its chances in the approaching 1932 elections. The painful memory of how the vigorous financial activity of the Poincaré ministry in 1924 had resulted in the defeat of his supporters and the coming to power of the *Cartel des Gauches* also explains why very little in the way of cutting expenses was achieved at this time.[23]

War debts and reparations.—In July, 1931 the French fiscal outlook was weakened still further when the Congress of the United States ratified the " Hoover moratorium " which called for a one-year suspension of all international war debts and reparations in view of the world depression. An immediate consequence for France was a drop of more than three billion francs in anticipated receipts,[24] which represented France's

22 Lachapelle, *op. cit.*, pp. 150-151.

23 *La France économique en 1931*, pp. 602-603.

24 $125,000,000; French fiscal employees used the figure of two billion francs, however, because some of the payments were to have been " in kind," and for budgetary purposes these were " marked down."

share of reparations payments worked out according to the Young Plan of January 20, 1930. Another outcome of this moratorium was the international conference which met at Lausanne in June, 1932 to consider a final settlement of the war debts-reparations problem in the face of Germany's insistence that the depression had rendered her unable to continue reparations payments.

The attitude of the United States toward this conference was most uncertain. In spite of Hoover's previous assurance to Laval that the United States would " cooperate " in a definitive settlement of " political " international indebtedness, Congress had expressly stated that the moratorium did not mean that the United States would surrender its right to be repaid for wartime loans.[25] The American government, in fact, did not even send an observer to the Lausanne Conference.

The governments represented at Lausanne had quite divergent ideas as to how the problem should be settled. England was most anxious that Germany be relieved of further reparations obligations; the English hoped that this would prevent further defaulting on their loans to Germany, defaulting which had already seriously involved the City in the financial panic of August and September, 1931. Italy wanted war debts and reparations wiped out together, since Italy's obligations to the United States and to England were much greater than any reparations she could expect from Germany.

The French delegation, on the other hand, obstinately refused to write off reparations. Georges Bonnet and Germain-Martin, the chief French representatives, held that to do so would imply absolving Germany of war guilt and furthermore would involve no guarantee of American generosity in a reciprocal cancellation of inter-Allied war debts.[26] A compro-

---

25 Germain-Martin, *op. cit.*, pp. 190-192.

26 *Ibid.*, p. 202. The French attitude was that the " Hoover moratorium " had as one of its major aims the rescue of tremendous American investments in Germany. *Le Temps*, June 29, 1931.

mise was finally worked out by which Germany would deposit three billion gold marks [27] in government-guaranteed bonds with the Bank for International Settlements; this was to be the last of the reparations payments.[28]

Another outcome of the Conference of Lausanne was the famous " Gentlemen's Agreement " by France, Italy, Belgium, and England on July 2, 1932. This agreement stipulated that the reparations settlement would not go into effect unless ratified by "interested powers." This meant that Germany's creditors would not surrender all but three billion marks of their claims to reparations unless they could conclude a " satisfactory " arrangement with their own creditors: i.e., the United States. The Conference of Lausanne and the " Gentlemen's Agreement," therefore, in effect not only settled German reparations but also cancelled the remaining "political " World War I debts, as far as the signatories were concerned.[29] From now on France could balance the loss of German reparations against the knowledge that " morally," at least, she was under no obligation to repay most of the war loans from the United States.

Depression warnings.—While the discussions on war debts and reparations were proceeding, French immunity to the world-wide depression was proving to have been only a temporary phenomenon. In November, 1930 a threatened financial panic had been staved off by the government when Paul Reynaud, Minister of Finance, had arranged with the Bank of France to support several bankrupt Paris and provincial banks until they could reopen their doors.[30] Debates on the proposed

27 $750,000,000.

28 This obligation was formally repudiated by Hitler in 1937.

29 In 1932, however, Great Britain and Italy made war debt payments in full to the United States; in 1933 these countries made " token " payments. In 1934 and thereafter only Finland persisted in war debt payments to the United States.

30 *JO, Débats, Chambre,* 1930, pp. 3427-3428; and Germain-Martin, *op. cit.,* p. 83.

budget for 1932 began to assume a rather hysterical tone as various government agencies and legislative commissions predicted higher and higher deficits. That the deficit was held down as low as 4.6 billion francs for the 1932 budget was due partly to the return to a fiscal year corresponding to the calendar year. Although the government declared that this step was taken in order to coordinate the budgetary years with payment of direct taxes (which had remained on a calendar basis), an immediate result was to spread twelve months of receipts from direct taxes over only nine months of total expenditures. This represented a decrease of perhaps 1.8 billions in the deficit for 1932.[31]

By the time the budget for 1933 came under discussion, the depression had made itself felt in every phase of French economic and financial life. Preliminary estimates for the deficit of this budget ranged from 12 billion francs according to the ministers of finance and the budget to 14.5 billions according to a legislative budget committee.[32]

The government then asked for a reduction of 2.6 billion francs in the estimated budget expenditures and for 1.5 billions of new receipts; the legislature refused to grant higher taxes but did reduce expenditures by 2.2 billion francs. The Treasury was also able to bring to a successful conclusion the eighteen-month-old debates on a proposed obligatory conversion of 5 and 6 per cent *rentes* to a new 4½ per cent seventy-five year *rente*. This resulted in a further saving of 1.4 billion francs for the 1933 budget.[33] More and more economists and financiers joined in urging higher taxes and retrenchment on the French legislature. "The budget must be balanced!" became the slogan of the day.

31 *Ibid.*, p. 96.

32 *La France économique en 1932*, pp. 676-677.

33 Germain-Martin, *op. cit.*, p. 180.

The fundamental question, [said Frédéric Jenny, the financial editor of *Le Temps,*] that to which all other financial problems are subordinated, is the question of equilibrium. The normal functioning of the Treasury, public credit, confidence of the country in the future of its finances and its money, all are linked closely to a solid equilibrium of receipts and expenditures of the State.[34]

In the confused and threatening situation in 1932 this was the one aspect of fiscal policy which emerged unquestioned. The atmosphere of confidence and self-satisfaction of the years 1927 to 1931 dissipated rapidly, leaving in its place an anxious quest for the monetary and fiscal measures which, it was assumed, had saved France during the crisis of 1926 and had provided her with the lush years 1928, 1929, and 1930. The groundwork for a transformation of this attitude into monetary policy had been laid as far back as the debates on the 1930-1931 budget:

If we make imprudent commitments now, their fulfillment will ruin public finances. . . . . The very basis of financial restoration, absolutely essential—and nobody will contradict me on this—is budgetary equilibrium. . . . From the day when that equilibrium is destroyed and our budgets show a deficit all the work of financial rehabilitation will disappear, because the foundation itself will be shaken.[35]

Here was the origin of the program of deliberate deflation which was to dominate the next phase of French fiscal and monetary policy.

THE " GOLDEN GLOW "—FRENCH BUSINESS CONDITIONS 1929-1932

" Whatever the causes of the world depression," announced the financial chronicler of *Le Temps* on August 18, 1930, " France can face it with relative serenity." The date is sig-

34 *Le Temps*, August 22, 1932.
35 Henry Chéron, in *JO, Débats, Chambre*, 1929, pp. 3104-3105.

nificant. Almost one year after the beginning of the most drastic and widespread depression of recent history, France still seemed to be comparatively immune. The problems facing French monetary authorities as a result of the depression were not the same as those presented to the governments of Great Britain, Germany, or the United States. As the business cycle worked itself out in France, it did not follow the " boom-and-bust " pattern apparent in many other countries. There was no clearly defined movement from " peak " to " trough," and the dates of the " turning points " of this period are singularly difficult to establish.[36]

After attaining the heights of prosperity in 1928-1929, the French economy showed a stubborn reluctance to follow the rest of the world down toward depression. This lag was followed, however, by a severe depression in France which lasted longer than in other countries. In a similar manner fiscal affairs continued to be satisfactory for a time after the beginning of the world depression, but budgetary surpluses accumulated in 1928 and 1929 disappeared in a flurry of deficits and Treasury crises in the following years. With the exception of a relatively minor and rapidly contained banking panic at the end of 1930, the French financial world remained comparatively untroubled until 1931; it then became the victim of a series of unresolved difficulties and " crises de confiance " which lasted until the overthrow of the Popular Front.

Industrial production.—The sequence of " boom—sustained boom—bust—stagnation " which was peculiar to France during this period can be seen in the general indexes of economic conditions, and particularly in those of industrial production. The recession in French industry in 1927 had proved to be a slight and temporary reaction to stabilization of the franc at the end of 1926. In 1928 industrial production resumed its expansive trend. But at this point French and world industrial production got out of step. There were apparently some factors

36 Burns and Mitchell, *op. cit.*, p. 113.

in France's recent economic and financial experience which enabled French industry to resist contraction until one year after industry in other countries had succumbed. One observer saw in this phenomenon the possibility that the United States soon might be displaced from her position of economic leadership of the world.[37]

GENERAL INDEXES OF INDUSTRIAL PRODUCTION [38]

(1925–1929 = 100)

	1925	1926	1927	1928	1929	1930	1931	1932
France	88	103	90	104	114	115	102	79
United Kingdom ..	99	76	109	104	112	100	85	86
Germany	89	85	107	109	110	97	79	66
United States	95	99	97	101	109	88	74	58

France was the only nation of the four listed whose level of industrial production was substantially as high in 1930 as in 1929. The above statistics reveal, moreover, that while industrial production in the United Kingdom suffered a decline of 24 per cent between 1929 and 1931, that in Germany a drop of 28 per cent, and that in the United States a drop of 32 per cent, in France general industrial production fell off by only 10 per cent. In 1932, however, French industrial production precipitously declined to a trough in July. A mild recovery which began in the fall of 1932 and lasted until the summer of 1933 was soon choked off. In 1934 the index of industrial production fell again to the depression level of 1932, and French industry began a period of stagnation which lasted until the nation became embroiled in the Second World War.[39]

Within the French industrial complex slackening of production developed at different rates for various sectors. Textile manufacture was one of the first hit, closely followed by the

37 *La France économique en 1929*, p. 666.

38 League of Nations, *World Production and Prices, 1925-1932* (Geneva, 1933), pp. 45, 49.

39 *SGF*, Index of Industrial Production, 1913 = 100.

automobile industry, chemicals, and the leather-goods trade.[40] Pig iron production reached a peak in October, 1929 and then began to decline, though at a much slower rate than had been the case during the recession of 1920-1921.[41] On the other hand, the production of electrical and mechanical equipment and paper goods continued to increase until May or June, 1930, and there were hardly any signs of decline in the rubber goods industry or in the building trades until 1932. These divergent movements offset each other enough so that the general index of industrial production throughout 1930 seemed to indicate continued stability.

This lag in the response of French industry to the Great Depression may not be dismissed as an aspect of the greater resistance of the French economy to cyclical fluctuations in general. In the world-wide business cycle of 1920-1921 the amplitude of the French industrial recession (29 per cent from peak to trough) was substantially equal to that of the American recession (32 per cent). And if France was less sensitive to the 1937-1938 depression than was the United States, the extent of the decline of American production at that time was unique among the industrialized nations of the world.

The 1930 lag in France was also remarkable for its length. While it is true that in recent years French fluctuations in industrial production have lagged behind those of the United States, the duration of the 1930 lag (about a year) greatly exceeded the three or four months lag observed in the cycles 1920-1922 and 1937-1939.

The French price structure and the Great Depression.—The same lag followed by an accentuated drop is shown by the general indexes of wholesale prices in France. The details of the wholesale index of forty-five articles demonstrate that prices of goods produced in France declined less quickly and less drastically than prices of goods imported into France. Fur-

40 *Ibid.*

41 NBER i, 189.

thermore, a definitive turning point for retail prices was not reached until twenty-two months after wholesale prices plunged downward.

TABLE 4

TURNING POINTS IN FRENCH PRICE INDEXES OF THE *SGF*

	Turning Point	Percentage Change		
		1929	1930	1931
Wholesale prices of industrial products (new index)	May, 1928	— 8	—21	—21
Wholesale prices of imported products (old index)	May, 1928	—19	—24	—15
General wholesale prices (new index) ..	Feb., 1929	— 9	— 6	—18
Wholesale prices of national products (old index)	May, 1929	— 3	— 7	—17
Retail prices (new index)	Dec., 1930	+ 2	+ 6	—14
Wholesale prices of foodstuffs (new index)	April, 1931	—10	+11	—15

There are two general indexes of wholesale prices calculated by the *Statistique Générale* for these years. The older index is based on July, 1914, and is the unweighted mean of forty-five articles. Among its drawbacks are the distant base year, the lack of weighting, and the small number of items used (twenty farm products and twenty-five raw and semi-finished industrial materials). This index is further divided into "nationally-produced" and "imported" materials and also into "industrial materials" and "foodstuffs." Extreme care is necessary in making observations based on either the older general index or its categories, for the "nationally-produced" category on examination proves to be almost exclusively foodstuffs and other agricultural produce, while the "imported" category is mainly composed of goods which have world-wide markets (tin, copper, lead, coffee, rubber, cotton, etc.), precisely the sort of goods which falls first and worst in depressions.

Thus the "imported products" index does not really lend itself to a comparison of French and foreign price trends, and

French contemporaries who used this index for such a comparison were in error.[42] The only conclusion about French price trends which we can reach on the basis of the general index of wholesale articles (and its components) is that food and other farm products remained at a higher price level than did the prices of industrial materials. But this in itself is a significant development, since in the United States it was the price of foods and farm products on which the depression had the most drastic effect. In France the decline in the prices of manufactured articles was less than that of raw materials and more than that of farm products.

Another, more recent wholesale price index of the *SGF* seems much more satisfactory: it is based on 126 articles, including 32 foodstuffs. This index is weighted by value in 1913, which is its base year.

The *SGF* also has calculated two indexes of retail prices, both based on July, 1914. The older index has only thirteen articles, eleven of which are foodstuffs; the newer index is not much more satisfactory, since it consists of only thirty-four articles, twenty-nine of which are foodstuffs. The fluctuations of the retail index, therefore, follow those of the wholesale agricultural index with little variation.

For a more meaningful approach to the problem of the lag in the effect of the world depression on French prices, we may compare the newer, 126 article index (which is not broken down into the " imported " and " national " categories of the older index) to the American Bureau of Labor Statistics index of wholesale prices.[43] The French wholesale price index and

---

42 See, for example, Bertrand Nogaro, *La Crise économique dans le monde et en France* (Paris: Librairie générale de droit et de jurisprudence, 1936), p. 245, and *La France économique en 1930*, p. 565.

43 This procedure, rather than an " imported-national " comparison, was suggested by Albert Aftalion in his work criticizing the quantity theorists' approach to the problem of the relatively high French price levels; *L'Or et sa distribution mondiale* (Paris: Dalloz, 1932), pp. 118 ff. Aftalion wrote before the newer wholesale price index was available.

CHART 4. COMPARISON OF FRENCH AND AMERICAN PRICE TRENDS, 1928-1934

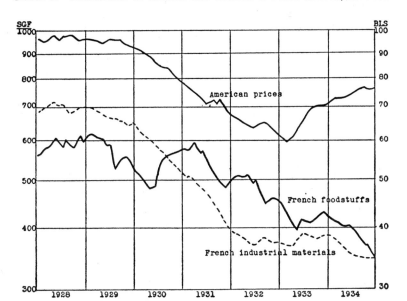

SOURCE: France, *SGF*, components of General Index of Wholesale
Prices of 126 articles, 1913 = 100. United States, wholesale price index of the BLS, 1926 = 100.

its component index of industrial materials and manufactured
products, we find, followed the course of the BLS index fairly
closely in the slight down-turn of 1929 and the more rapid
decline of 1930.[44]

The agricultural products component of the French index,
however, followed an erratic, independent path after the spring
of 1930. From February, 1929 to April, 1930, both the agricultural and the industrial products indexes fell at about the
same rate—25 per cent. But beginning in the spring of 1930
the agricultural price index bounded upward; it continued to
climb until April, 1931, reaching a peak at an index of 592,

44 See Chart 4.

only 4 per cent lower than the prosperity peak of February, 1929.[45]

From January, 1930 to April, 1931 wheat at Paris rose from 133 to 188 francs per 100 kilograms and potatoes from 42 to 135 francs per 100 kilograms. During the same period the price of Winnipeg wheat delivered in London fell 51 per cent, and even in ultra-protectionist Germany there was a drop in the price of wheat.[46]

In the summer and fall of 1930 there was a severe drought which ruined a large fraction of the crops; the wheat crop was especially hard hit. And in 1931 the French legislature rushed to the defense of its rural constituents and instituted a quota system for imports of agricultural commodities to forestall competition from other nations, who almost without exception found themselves with low-priced farm products begging for a market.[47] But ever-higher tariffs and more stringent quotas [48] proved incapable of protecting French agriculture after the spring of 1931. Except for a brief recovery of agricultural prices in the spring of 1932, and another in the spring of 1933, the tendency of farm prices was steadily downward; between April, 1931 and December, 1932, the index of agricultural prices fell from 592 to 456, a slump of 23 per cent. It was at this point that the prices of American farm products began to recover; but French agricultural prices continued on their downward path until the summer of 1935.

Income and employment.—The vogue of the quantity theory of money in France at this time was enhanced by the extra-

45 During the same period the foods and farm products components of the BLS wholesale index fell between 30 and 40 per cent.

46 *La France économique en 1930*, p. 496.

47 The origins of the French quota system for imports can be found in this desire of the legislature to protect the French agricultural community. See Haight, *op. cit.*, p. 165. With the exception of coal, which was protected by a quota after June, 1931, it was not until 1932 that the quota system was extended to industrial materials and manufactured goods.

48 Especially directed against imports from the sterling bloc countries after the devaluation of the pound sterling in 1931.

ordinary behavior of French agricultural prices in 1930-1931. If changes in prices are due to changes in the ratio of goods to money, reasoned the adherents of this theory, then surely high agricultural prices originated in the vast amount of money and capital in France on the one hand and the shortage of foods (because of the drought and import restrictions) on the other.[49] According to this viewpoint high prices, in turn, acted as a brake on the progress of the business recession. But such emphasis on prices rather than income puts effect before cause.

The plentiful supply of gold, currency, and credit, however it impressed contemporary bankers and economists, could not itself generate a high level of national income. In fact much of the money transferred to Paris after the stabilization of the franc remained outside the flow of income, being transferred from foreign to domestic banks without affecting French business activity.[50] Nevertheless it is true that French national income was kept at prosperity heights until 1932. It is in this phenomenon, and not in the quantity of money, that the key is found to the explanation of continued prosperity and high prices after 1929.

According to the estimates of Dugé de Bernonville, French national income was virtually as high in 1930 as in 1929 (243 and 245 billion francs, respectively). Although there was a serious decline to 229 billion francs in 1931, this figure is still two billion francs higher than that for the prosperity year

49 Institut scientifique de Recherches économiques et sociales, *Tableaux de l'économie française, 1910-1934* (Paris: Recueil Sirey, 1935), explanation accompanying Charts 5 and 11.

50 Presumably, the capital inflow could have affected business activity by lowering interest rates and thus stimulating investment. But interest rates in the Paris money-market were already quite low—much lower than those of the financial centers from which the funds were coming. In the parlance of international economics, these capital movements were of a "disequilibrating" nature, since they acted to aggravate, rather than to adjust, differences in interest rates from one country to another.

1928.[51] By way of contrast, personal income in the United States declined from 85 billion dollars in 1929 to 65 billions in 1931, or about 24 per cent, while French income fell only 7 per cent.

Along with a high level of income France enjoyed a comparatively high level of employment. In 1932, when one-third of the total labor force was suffering unemployment in the United States and in Germany, in France less than 2 per cent of the total occupied population was on public relief rolls. It is true that the French statistics on " chomeurs secourus " do not take into account partial unemployment, workers refused assistance, or those not requesting assistance. It is also true that some unemployment in France not accounted for by French statistics was at the expense of foreign laborers. With a birth rate too low for her needs, France in recent years has been provided with a " safety valve " in the ability of the government to increase or decrease the number of foreign laborers in France almost at will. The net movement of foreign workers is thus a useful indication of French business conditions. It affords us more proof that 1930 and 1931 were comparatively good years; in 1930 there was an influx of about 178,000 foreign workers, considerably more than in 1929. It was not until 1932 that the net movement of foreign workers was in an outward direction.

Another indication that France was spared for a time from the most painful onslaughts of the depression is to be found in wage statistics. The average daily wage of French coal miners, for example, rose from 30.69 francs at the beginning of 1928 to 36.70 francs at the end of 1929, and continued to rise until the end of 1930, when it stood at 37.16 francs.[52]

51 In terms of stable (1938) prices, Froment and Gavanier estimate that French national income declined from 391 billion francs in 1929 to 369 in 1931. In current francs, these estimates are about 30 per cent higher than those of Dugé de Bernonville. See Appendix II.

52 *SGF.*

Unfortunately, we are unable to separate out statistically which portions of the increase in French national income at this time were linked to the current balance of payments and which to other factors, such as domestic expansion. But since the multiplier effects of current balances may take a year or more to work their way through the economy, we may see in the huge current surpluses of 1928 and 1929 a powerful contribution to the maintenance of French income at high levels in 1930 and 1931.

The characteristic structure of French trade itself is sometimes given as one of the reasons behind the lag in the French recession. The major part of French imports were raw materials, while her exports were heavily weighted toward services and consumers' goods. The depression affected first of all the volume and the prices of capital goods; consumers' goods and services at first remained relatively unaffected. This also accounts for the high level of French invisible exports in 1930 and 1931.

While the price of French commodity exports remained higher than the price of goods imported into the country, the *volume* of French exports suffered heavily from the contraction of foreign business activity. There was an instant worsening of the French balance of commodity trade after the beginning of the depression. This item had always been negative, but all through the 1920's (apart from 1920 itself) it was kept at a relatively small magnitude—always less than five billion Poincaré francs and virtually nothing in 1921, 1924, and 1927. But in 1929 the negative balance of commodity trade rose to over eleven billion francs, and continued to rise until 1932, when it declined slightly to ten billion francs. The quantum index of French trade [59] (1927 = 100) shows that while imports increased steadily after 1928 to 131.2 in 1930 and remained as high as 129.4 in 1931 (when they were at a higher

59 League of Nations, *Review of World Trade, 1938* (Geneva, 1939), p. 76.

level than in 1929), exports declined from 101.4 in 1928 to 76.7 in 1931. In 1932 the quantum index of imports was at 108.3, still considerably higher than in the base year 1927, while exports had fallen to the very low index of 58.9. While national income remained high enough so that the French imported about the same quantity of goods as during prosperity, France's export markets were shrinking away.

The result was that in 1931 a deficit in the balance of payments on current account appeared for the first time since 1920. Because of " reverse multiplier " effects, French national income now suffered a decline greater in magnitude than the negative balance of payments. While other nations began to experience some improvement in their national income after 1932, in France income declined each year until 1936.

The golden avalanche.—These developments in income and trade, however, received scant consideration in France at this time. The attention of most observers was riveted on the spectacular flow of gold and money to France. Even to those Frenchmen unacquainted with the more sophisticated aspects of the quantity theory of money, the presence of both continued prosperity and vastly larger supplies of gold and money seemed more than a coincidence. One observer even spoke of " monetary saturation " and " excessive credit " and wondered if in time a harmfully high French price level might not be the result.[60]

GOLD RESERVES AT THE BANK OF FRANCE [61]

June, 1928	....	5.9 billion francs (before devaluation)
June, 1929	....	36.6 billion francs
June, 1930	....	43.9 billion francs
June, 1931	....	56.3 billion francs
June, 1932	....	81.2 billion francs

60 *La France économique en 1930*, p. 565.

61 *SGF.* These vast increases in French gold reserves, moreover, represented a *net increase* to reserves at the Bank of France, since during the flight from the franc in 1925 and 1926 France had been off the gold standard and had preserved the Bank's gold reserves virtually intact. Economists

When the flow of gold toward France became large enough to be a matter for concern to other nations, France was accused of causing a "maldistribution" of the world's gold and thus endangering the whole international gold standard system. The Bank of France answered these criticisms by announcing serenely that the flow of gold toward France was in no way a result of interference with foreign money markets on the part of French monetary authorities; furthermore, the gold might some day leave France and would be allowed to do so as freely as it had entered.[62] By 1932 there were about 5,000 metric tons of gold in the vaults of the Bank of France; without even accounting for France's large amounts of privately-hoarded gold,[63] this represented about one-fourth of the world's total gold supply.[64]

There is some evidence that the officials of the Bank of France regarded the later stages of this golden avalanche as rather a mixed blessing. The Bank did what it could to offset the drift of capital to France which was partly responsible for the inflow of gold;[65] discount and interest rates in Paris were kept low so as to make other financial centers more attractive to holders of liquid capital. The Treasury cooperated by liquidating its considerable holdings of foreign exchange only when

---

who placed great importance on international gold movements saw in this extraordinary flow of gold to France a contribution to the world-wide monetary deflation after 1929. *Cf.* Gustav Cassel, *The Downfall of the Gold Standard* (Oxford: Clarendon Press, 1936), pp. 60-62.

62 Sédillot, *op. cit.*, p. 342. In effect, the Bank invoked the concept of "automatic" monetary law.

63 In 1929 and 1930 a small fraction of France's privately-hoarded gold—something less than one billion francs—was "dishoarded" due to an increasing willingness to hoard notes instead of gold.

64 Pirou, *Traité*, p. 237. In 1926 the Bank had held only 8 per cent of the world's gold reserves.

65 The other major factor, of course, was the favorable balance of payments on current account. See Appendix III for rough estimates of the volume of "hot money" which entered France during these years.

forced to do so, taking care meanwhile to order these operations so as to place the least possible pressure on foreign currencies.[66]

Those who blamed the Bank of France for short-sighted selfishness in gathering too large a share of the world's precious metal were inclined to disregard the fact that after 1929, and until the pound sterling was devalued in 1931, the Bank did not liquidate any further large amounts of its foreign exchange reserves.[67] The Bank's power to buy foreign exchange was cancelled by the monetary law of June, 1928, and thereafter the Bank could not use purchase and sale of foreign currencies as a means of enlarging its gold reserves.[68] While the Bank's foreign exchange reserves remained fairly constant between 1928 and 1931, however, its gold reserves continued to climb.

	Foreign Exchange Reserves [69]	Gold Reserves [70]
	(billions of francs)	(billions of francs)
June, 1929	26.0	36.6
December, 1929	26.0	41.1
June, 1930	25.5	43.9
December, 1930	26.0	53.0
June, 1931	26.0	56.3
August, 1931	26.5	58.6
December, 1931	22.5	68.3
December, 1932	4.5	83.2
December, 1933	1.0	77.1

66 Aftalion, *op. cit.*, pp. 223-225.

67 Paul Einzig, for example, claims that the flow of gold from London to Paris was turned on and off whenever France wanted to put pressure on Great Britain in political matters. *World Finance, 1919-1935* (New York: Macmillan Co., 1935), p. 174. The French Treasury did unload about 7.5 billion francs in foreign exchange during 1930 and 1931, but for the purpose of meeting budgetary deficits rather than to influence political decisions.

68 Between July, 1928 and the end of the year, however, the Bank increased its foreign exchange holdings from 29.5 to 33.0 billion francs as a result of settling forward exchange commitments made before the passage of the monetary law.

69 *L'Evolution de l'économie française*, Table 41.

70 *SGF.*

The Bank of France itself, therefore, did not contribute to the pressure on the Bank of England during the panic of September, 1931, which resulted in the suspension of gold convertibility in Great Britain. Both the Bank of France and the Federal Reserve System, in fact, tried to help the British central bank by refusing to convert their sterling holdings and by negotiating loans of 650 million dollars to their opposite number in Britain.[71]

On the other hand privately-held French funds in England, considerable amounts of which had fled there in the post-war era and had remained even after the stabilization of the franc, now scurried across the Channel into the haven offered by French banks. Furthermore, the shaky financial situation after 1929 and the failure of a few minor French banks in 1930 induced the large commercial banks to make their position as liquid as possible so as to be able to cope with the possibility of a "run." The commercial banks therefore liquidated their foreign exchange reserves after 1929 and greatly increased their ratio of cash to deposits.[72]

The British devaluation meant a loss of 2.3 billion francs to the Bank of France on its sterling holdings (later reimbursed by the French Treasury),[73] and many other French financial institutions lost heavily.[74] The lesson of the "bankruptcy" of the pound sterling now caused financiers to scrutinize anxiously their holdings in the United States. "Hot money" began to stream out of New York in 1932, bound for Paris; within a few months gold convertibility in the United States was

71 Wolff, *op. cit.*, p. 151. Similar help was given the Reichsbank at this time.

72 W. H. Wynne, "The French Franc, June, 1928—February, 1937," *Journal of Political Economy*, August, 1937, p. 492. The ratio of cash holdings to deposits at the "Big Four" commercial banks increased from 7.5 per cent in June, 1929 to 32.6 per cent in November, 1931.

73 Myers, *op. cit.*, pp. 94-96.

74 Lachapelle, *op. cit.*, p. 171.

suspended, and eventually the dollar was devalued by 40 per cent in terms of gold. The Paris money-market now became the principal center for international operations in gold.

Money and exchange rates.—One of the most striking aspects of the period 1929-1932 was a tremendous rise in the volume of currency and bank deposits in France, which of course was associated with the inflow of gold and capital. Thus the tendency toward monetary expansion was continued in France when other countries were experiencing severe deflations. In Chapter II we saw how the influx of gold which followed the stabilization of the franc in 1926 was partly neutralized by the reduction of currency in circulation due to the repayment of the Bank of France's loans to the State. But the situation after 1929 did not allow such offsetting actions, and as a result the monetary and credit structure of France was greatly altered.

TABLE 5

TREND OF MONEY AND DEPOSITS, 1928–1932 *

(Billions of francs—end-of-the-year data)

	Savings Banks Deposits	Current Accounts and Time and Demand Deposits (other than govt.) at the Bank of France	Bank-notes in Circulation	Current Accounts and Demand Deposits, " Big Four " Banks	Current Accounts and Demand Deposits, 21 Private Banks
1928	27.0	6.5	62.3	34.4	24.5
1929	32.0	7.0	67.4	32.8	25.8
1930	38.6	10.0	75.7	34.2	24.2
1931	50.9	23.5	83.5	36.8	23.1
1932	57.3	21.5	83.6	36.5	20.5

* Sources: *La France économique* and *L'Evolution de l'économie française*, Table 39.

The rise in bank-notes in circulation over this period was greatly exceeded by the increases in the gold reserves of the central bank: 21.3 billion francs for bank-notes as against 51.4 billion francs in the gold reserves. After the devaluation of the pound sterling the Bank rapidly liquidated most of its remaining reserves of foreign exchange, to the amount of 28.5 billion francs between December, 1928 and December, 1932. This in effect merely represented a shift in the internationally negotiable assets of the Bank from foreign currencies to gold. The remainder of the increases in the Bank's gold reserves— 22.9 billion francs, which resulted from the continued inflow of refuge-seeking capital—went to swell the amount of Bank of France notes in circulation.

The private individuals who transferred "hot money" to France either invested in short-term government securities or deposited their funds with the Bank of France or the savings banks. Table 5 shows a great increase in deposits at the savings banks and at the Bank of France, but no significant increase in the deposits of the "Big Four" or other banks which make the bulk of the commercial loans.

The inflow of capital after 1929, therefore, had little or no expansive effect on French business. It was brought to France for security, and necessarily remained liquid. By being physically present in France, on the other hand, it bloated the money-market. The financial panics of the fall of 1929 in New York, the spring of 1931 in Central Europe, and the late summer of 1931 in London had almost no counterpart in Paris. Apart from a relatively unimportant flurry of bank failures at the end of 1930, a situation which was promptly shored up by the government and the Bank of France, the Paris money-market remained quite calm. Stock market speculation had never reached the same proportions in Paris as in other financial centers, and while stock prices on the Paris Bourse declined after the 1929 New York crash, until the end of 1930 the magnitude of the drop was not at all comparable to the collapse of stock prices in New York.

INDEX OF STOCK PRICES [75]

(1913 = 100)

April, 1928	413	October, 1930	395
October, 1928	450	April, 1931	346
April, 1929	518	October, 1931	249
October, 1929	489	April, 1932	250
April, 1930	486	October, 1932	227

The discount rate in French banks remained steady and low during the first part of the depression, reflecting this absence of financial panic. All through 1928, 1929, 1930, and 1931, the bank rate in Paris was lower than that in London.[76] The rate of short-term loans fell steadily, and was consistently lower than that of New York or of London. On January 2, 1931 the Bank of France reduced its discount rate to 2 per cent, at that time the lowest rate in its history. The monthly value of new issues of French stocks and bonds offered in Paris, furthermore, continued to increase until the end of 1930, and did not fall below the 1928 level until the summer of 1932.[77]

Reversing the situation of the early 1920's, the franc now was the stable currency, and its exchange rate increased sharply in terms of pounds and dollars. Three-month forward sterling in Paris was at a discount through most of 1929 and 1930 and through all of 1931. After the abandonment of the gold standard by Great Britain, the franc rose from 124 per pound sterling in August, 1931 to 86 at the end of the year. When the dollar was taken off gold the franc rose from 4 American cents to 6.6 cents. An influx of gold, a strong foreign exchange rate, a plentiful supply of money and deposits, low rates of interest—these were the characteristics of the French money-market during the first few years of the Great Depression.

75 NBER, 11,24.

76 Paul Einzig, *The Theory of Forward Exchange* (London: Macmillan Co., 1937), pp. 487-488.

77 NBER, 10,33.

The Aftermath of the Golden Glow

When considered in relation to the previous period of prosperity and stabilization and the following years of deep depression, the initial resistance of the French economy to the world depression is revealed as a phenomenon of debatable benefit to France. It was only a temporary respite, an interval of marking time while staving off the implacable future. And when depression did come, it continued to distress France after other countries had started on the road to recovery.

The sense of security which France derived from the huge gold reserves of the Bank of France was falsely placed, since only the *continued* relative degree of French prosperity and financial stability could assure the continued presence of the precious metal. After 1932 it was evident that France was to have its share of the depression. Until the devaluation of the dollar, unsettled conditions in other financial centers kept this "hot money" in Paris. Once it became apparent, however, not only that France was entering a period of depression, but also that other countries were beginning to recover, the "capital migrateur" left with a rush.

The monetary developments of 1929 to 1931 were completely misinterpreted by the French authorities, who saw a direct and causal relationship between the size of France's gold reserves, the stability of the franc, and the absence of budgetary deficits. The first uneasy glimmerings of concern for budgetary stability at the time of the "disorders wrought by years of budgetary facility" finally became a desperate reliance on fiscal equilibrium as the only salvation for France. In a sense this was a continuation of the financial policies of the Poincaré ministry. The inflation of the early 1920's had been blamed on excessive governmental expenditures, and the stabilization achieved by Poincaré was attributed to his ability to contain the budget within the limits of tax receipts. The experience of the years 1926 to 1928 seemed to confirm the attitude of

French economists and statesmen that a national budget was to be regarded as a large-scale counterpart of a private budget, in which an excess of outlay over income was regarded as a disaster. One strange result of "l'expérience Poincaré" was that by its very success it prevented future financial leaders of France from realizing that steps taken to ameliorate a situation involving rising prices might not necessarily be applicable in times of falling prices.

After continued warnings on the importance of budgetary stability, the financial "brains" now began to insist upon it. At a certain point—when the deficits wiped out the Treasury's revenue surpluses accumulated from more prosperous years—the legislature gave in. The transition to a policy of deflation was the result.

Thus we have the beginnings of a situation in France in which those in control of financial affairs became more and more convinced of the urgent necessity of raising taxes and lowering expenditures. Meanwhile the objective situation made this policy more difficult of realization each month, and its stubborn application may have had, in the long run, some retardative effect on France's recovery from the depression. Between 1926 and 1933 a large body of opinion in France became fanatically concerned with the symbol of budgetary equilibrium. The answer of men of this conviction to the problems of depression and the difference between French and international prices was deliberate deflation. Paradoxically, productive measures like the program for refurnishing *outillage national,* which would now be acceptable as anti-depression measures, were voted by the French legislature during the early 1930's as political measures. They were regarded as extremely harmful by those in charge of the monetary policy of the country.

In the next phase of the monetary history of France, from 1932 until 1936, the action of these advocates of deflation in limiting expenditures and lowering prices and income aggravated the vicious cycle of deflation and depression; France did not "touch bottom" in the depression until 1935.

CHAPTER IV
DEPRESSION AND DEFLATION
THE FIGHT TO SAVE THE GOLD FRANC, 1933-1936

THE " politico-financial hegemony " which France had enjoyed on the Continent since the establishment of the Poincaré régime in 1926 was greatly weakened by 1933. The existence of the Nazi dictatorship was a direct challenge to France's political leadership, and the difficulties caused by the world depression undermined her position in economic and financial matters. Fiscal problems, especially, became increasingly serious, until they finally developed into a prime concern of French political life as they had been ten years previously. An atmosphere of financial crisis dominated the affairs of the Fifteenth Legislature almost from its inception in 1932. The main problem—continued budgetary deficits—was posed against a background of serious business depression. The solution advanced by almost every French government until the advent of the Popular Front was retrenchment, higher taxes, a budget to be balanced at all costs, lower price and wage levels: briefly, budgetary curtailment and deliberate price deflation became the fiscal and monetary policy of France.

This policy was never justified by appeal to an organized body of economic theory. And it is hardly possible to arrive at an integrated expression of it by reference to the measures which were passed in its name. A dreadful welter of contradictory financial and economic laws and decrees was visited on France between the years 1933 and 1936. But one policy was almost unanimously approved: *the budget must be balanced.* None of the French governments or parties dared question this dictum. What we now call " deficit financing " was then known as " national bankruptcy." While prices fell and industrial activity slumped, while unstable ministries were struggling with dangerous social and political disorders, the attention of the financial and political leadership of France remained rigidly fixed upon the sanctified necessity of forcing governmental expenditures down to the dwindling level of revenue income. The first half-hearted attempts to cut expenses were for the most part successfully resisted by the legislature. But after the summer of 1933, when the world depression fastened more seriously on France, that frightened and bewildered country meekly gave way before the self-proclaimed " esprits informés " who advocated strenuous budgetary trimming and who pointed to the fiscal stability achieved by Poincaré in 1926 as proof that policies which had succeeded during that financial crisis would save the country again.

Complicating the whole issue was the problem of the " overvalued " franc. After the devaluations of the pound sterling and the dollar, the franc was worth more in terms of foreign currencies and gold than in terms of purchasing power within France. The discrepancy between French and British price levels has been estimated at about 10 per cent for the cost of living and 25 per cent for wholesale prices in 1933.[1] This meant that to importers in the sterling bloc and the dollar area French goods were now relatively dear. To all except the few advocates of a French devaluation, the solution to this problem was not to drive down the exchange value of the franc, but to drive down wages and prices within France to the point where French goods could compete again on international markets. The work of the downward swing of the business cycle in reducing national income was to be complemented by the reduction of national money income as a matter of policy.

No such unpopular aims were admitted, of course, by the advocates of deflation. In so far as they thought in terms of national income at all, for example, they claimed that a reduction of the national debt was necessary if entrepreneurs were to be encouraged. Since the uses to which taxes are put by the state are largely " sterile," it was argued, reduction of public

1 Estimate of the *Economist*, May 30, 1936, p. 492. The base period used is September, 1931. The overvaluation of the franc as regards American prices was considerably higher.

indebtedness and state expenses would thus *increase* national income by increasing the proportion left in the hands of private citizens.[2] Moreover, lowering wages, prices, and interest rates would stimulate industry by lowering costs of production.[3]

Ministerial instability and fiscal difficulties.—The theory of deflation represented by the above arguments was a relatively late development. The first stage was simply a reëmphasis on the necessity of balancing the budget. In 1932 the government of Herriot continued the attempt to achieve budgetary equilibrium begun, in a half-hearted way, by the preceding Tardieu and Laval ministries. But Herriot's slim and shifting parliamentary majority was not enough to pass his budget-stabilizing measures. After having cooperated to elect a Left majority, the Socialists, as in 1924, refused to give their complete support to the government. In December Herriot's government was defeated on its proposal to pay the coming installment of the World War I " political " debt to the United States.[4]

There followed in rapid succession five additional Radical governments: those of Paul-Boncour, Daladier, Sarraut, Chautemps, and again Daladier. Proposals for " redressement budgétaire " were for the most part defeated by the Chamber of Deputies as quickly as they were advanced, though the Senate was more inclined to accept some strong fiscal medicine. During 1933 five provisional " twelfths " (monthly outlays) had to be voted in order to furnish the State with funds while the budget for the whole year was being bitterly but inconclusively debated by the legislature. Meanwhile total governmental expenditures remained virtually as high as during prosperity, while tax receipts fell rapidly. The surplus accumulated by the Treasury during the more fortunate years was soon dissipated,

2 *Le Temps financier*, July 22, 1935, and Germain-Martin, *op. cit.*, pp. 336-337.

3 Olivier Wormser, *Déflation et Dévaluation, étude comparée de leurs effets sur les prix* (Paris: Recueil Sirey, 1938), pp. 38-42.

4 Maurice Baumont, *La Faillite de la paix (1918-1939)* (2d ed.; " Peuples et Civilisations "; Paris: Presses Universitaires, 1946), pp. 469-470.

and in 1933 the public debt rose from 291 to 302 billion francs. This was the first important increase in the public debt since 1928.

The failure of the London Economic Conference.—From the point of view of French fiscal policy during these years, one of the most disappointing incidents in international relations was the failure of the London Economic Conference, which was called in June, 1933 to discuss means of offsetting the world depression by international economic cooperation. From the beginning there were at least two clearly opposed bodies of opinion on measures to relieve the economic crisis. As far as the gold bloc countries were concerned, the purpose of this conference was " to stabilize currencies and to establish conditions necessary to the satisfactory functioning of a stable international monetary standard.[5] Within France, the financial community rallied around the gold standard and exhorted the government to stand firm:

> France . . . will maintain the gold standard. In the midst of universal upheaval, she will cling to the solid ground offered by monetary order, and her money will show other nations the sole road to follow and the sole goal to aim at in order for the world to recover normal activity and future security with sane currencies.[6]

But American delegates endorsed another point of view soon after the conference began, based on the position taken by President Roosevelt. He labelled arguments for reëstablishing international gold-based monetary stability as " worn-out fetishes of international bankers " and called upon the conference to discuss broader economic problems facing the world.[7] The Bank of England and the Bank for International

5 P. Belgrand, *De la Dévaluation de 1928 à la dévaluation de 1936* (Paris: Domat-Monchrestien, 1937), p. 22.

6 *Le Temps financier*, April 24, 1933.

7 H. V. Hodson, *Slump and Recovery, 1929-1937* (London: Oxford University Press, 1938), pp. 172 ff.

Settlements appeared to be ready to accept some fixed exchange relationship for the dollar, the franc, and the pound, but not a return to the old gold parities.[8]

Georges Bonnet, Minister of Finance and France's chief representative at this conference, seized the opportunity to emphasize France's insistence on gold as the only possible medium of international exchange. He blamed the continuation of the depression on the refusal of the paper-standard countries to " stabilize " their currencies; *i.e.,* to establish a fixed relationship to gold. According to the French, Roosevelt's insistence on enlarging the scope of discussions beyond purely monetary questions had ruined the chances of international economic cooperation. The conference was finally " adjourned," a complete failure.

In July, 1933, the governors of the central banks of France, Italy, Poland, Czechoslovakia, Holland, and Switzerland met in Paris for the formal establishment of the gold bloc. The signatories agreed, in a declaration drawn up at this meeting, to help each other to maintain the gold basis of their several monetary units and to resist further devaluations.[9]

Doumergue and the decree-laws.—Meanwhile, fiscal affairs in France were rapidly deteriorating. Each government in 1932 and 1933 proposed a more or less drastic series of measures to deal with the problem of insufficient tax receipts, only to have its program thrown out by the Chamber of Deputies. The government of Paul-Boncour, seeking to repeat Poincaré's success, asked a new " Committee of Experts " under Fournier, assistant governor of the Bank of France, to draw up new proposals for the " immediate reëstablishment of budgetary equilibrium, no matter how severe the sacrifice this im-

8 Cassell, *op. cit.,* pp. 150-153.

9 The only test made of the cooperative strength of the gold bloc was in March, 1935, when Belgium was faced by a run on her gold reserves. The Belgian government appealed to the Bank of France for help, was refused, and was overthrown by the Belgian legislature. The next ministry undertook a devaluation of the belga, which, however, remained a gold standard currency.

plies." [10] But the only result of the embodiment of the Experts' suggestions in legislative bills was the overthrow of the Paul-Boncour ministry.

The period of legislative indecision ended early in 1934. Political and social unrest caused by the business recession toward the end of 1933 was brought into sharp focus by the demoralizing Stavisky scandals in which several public figures were implicated. The bloody riots of February 6, 1934, involving both Fascist and Communist bands, seemed to call into question not only the present administration but also the whole parliamentary system of France. The frightened legislature was glad to accept a strong man in the person of seventy-one-year-old former President Gaston Doumergue, who came out of political retirement to reunite several political groups in a "Cabinet of National Union."

These serious events prompted another development of the theory of deflation. The emphasis of the reasons given for governmental fiscal measures shifted from a desire to balance the budget as an end in itself to a need to protect the financial world from loss of confidence in the franc. " Was it not a banking crisis which had ruined the dollar? " [11] Now extraordinary powers were given the government to " save the franc " by demonstrating France's ability to maintain the gold standard and to resist devaluation. The legislature allowed the administration to establish by decree having the force of law all necessary financial measures.

Doumergue opened his campaign of deflation by promulgating a 10 per cent slash in the salaries of all employees of government bureaus. The more highly-paid government functionaries were subjected to a further 5 to 10 per cent levy on their salaries. All civil and military pensions were reduced 3 per cent, except those for severely wounded veterans. All heads of governmental offices were instructed to make a thorough

10 Quoted in Lachapelle, *op. cit.*, p. 193.

11 Germain-Martin, *op. cit.*, p. 299.

check of their staffs and activities in the interests of " economy," and Doumergue asserted that 30,000 *fonctionnaires*
should be discharged as soon as possible. The government put
its seal of approval on the " Marquet Plan " to improve the
nation's railroad systems and to cut down on operating deficits, which were the responsibility of the State.[12] The legislative financial committees were told that in the 1935 budget,
whatever the needs of the State, expenditures were to be scaled
down to the level of estimated receipts.

Both Doumergue and his Minister of Finance, Germain-
Martin, firmly declared that the four-sou franc must be defended, come what may, against another devaluation. In a
" fireside chat " of March 24, 1934, Doumergue asked: " How
to balance the budget? In a State budget as in a private budget,
we must never have expenses higher than receipts. That is the
rule." Like a private family in reduced circumstances, said
Doumergue, the State must limit its *train de vie*.[13]

Shortly after Doumergue came to power, he had managed
to get the 1934 budget voted *en bloc* rather than by sections,
thus avoiding a repetition of the painfully drawn-out legislative
haggling over the 1933 budget. But in spite of his strenuous
attempts to balance the budget, tax receipts were lower than
the expenses of government in 1934 as well as in 1933. Items
of expense like servicing the public debt and national defense
were, of course, hardly compressible. The unquestioned need
to help the gravely augmented number of unemployed added
to public burdens. In spite of the " Marquet Plan," the deficit
of the nationalized railroad lines rose to four billion francs in
1934 and to four and one-half billions in 1935. Chiefs of governmental bureaus were reluctant to carry out the directives
on firing large numbers of employees, and the unions of government employees began a campaign against what *L'Human-
ité,* Communist newspaper, called Doumergue's " Famine
Plan."

12 *Ibid.*, pp. 258-266.

13 *Le Temps,* March 26, 1934.

The position of the French Treasury had become most alarming. Issues of Treasury bonds and *bons de la défense nationale* newly authorized by the legislature brought in barely enough funds to keep pace with the total value of old issues falling due.[14] Appeals by the government to the Bank of France and to private banks resulted only in counter-demands to balance the budget.

The Bank of France used its influence and its money to inspire a vigorous editorial campaign in the French press for a balanced budget and against devaluation.[15] The " Big Four " commercial banks also used whatever pressures they could command in behalf of a greater deflationary effort. Men whose chief concerns were that the gold standard be retained at all costs and that the French banking system be protected from any danger of panic scorned ideas which now seem basic tenets of fiscal policy. They could not understand that lower budgetary income was the inevitable result of strangulation of the country's economy, and that increasing taxes and limiting expenditures during a depression only aggravates the economic and the dependent financial situation.

By October, 1934 the *pleins-pouvoirs* given the French government had expired and the fiscal situation was becoming steadily worse. Doumergue then announced a plan to dissolve the Chamber of Deputies without the consent of the Senate, which if accomplished would be a step without precedent in the history of the Third Republic. In this way he would try to get a legislature which would support more drastic financial measures. But the abrupt resignation of several ministers in protest against the proposed " dictatorship " and the overthrow of his government sent Doumergue back into retirement, this time permanently.

The Flandin ministry.—The new government, formed November 8, 1934, was marked by a curious division of opinion regarding monetary policy. Germain-Martin, the previous

14 *La France économique en 1934*, pp. 670-671.

15 Wolff, *op. cit.*, p. 192.

Minister of Finance and a recognized bulwark of financial purity, was retained in his post from which, presumably, he could carry on the good fight for deflation. Flandin, himself, on the other hand, seems to have thought that deflation had gone far enough. As he announced to the Chamber of Deputies, he would not permit a devaluation and would continue to work for budgetary equilibrium, but there would be no further cuts in governmental expenditure. How, then, could the budget be balanced? Flandin believed the problem could be solved by relieving the strain on the money-market, lowering the long-term rate of interest, and promoting business recovery which would in turn enlarge governmental revenue.[16]

Many of the measures promulgated by the Flandin administration followed the usual pattern of deflationist thought. On January 10, 1935, the government was given powers to make regional and industrial cartels compulsory, provided that two-thirds of the producers and three-fourths of the total production was represented. This measure was designed mainly to help the very depressed textile industry; the government hoped that improved efficiency through cartelization would help bring down prices.[17] Flandin also did away with the government's wheat subsidy to relieve the budget of an additional burden and raised the compulsory school attendance age to fourteen to lessen unemployment.

In spite of these measures, Flandin's monetary policy came to be known as " reflationist " in certain circles which were bitterly opposed to his attitude toward the problem of budgetary deficits. These deficits meant that the Treasury was going to be forced to borrow, but Flandin took the stand that the borrowing should be done so as to spare the already overloaded money-market as much as possible. In brief, Flandin wanted the Bank of France to discount freely short-term Treasury bonds, in order to make these bonds more attractive

16 Lachapelle, *op. cit.*, p. 204.

17 Hodson, *op. cit.*, pp. 366-367. Meanwhile the United States, through the NRA, was promoting cartelization to raise prices!

to investors. The Bank resisted bitterly, claiming that this was a disguised form of Bank-to-State advances. Flandin replaced the governor of the Bank with one of his own choosing, but the Regents remained unswayed in their opinion that the only way to ease the money-market was more budgetary trimming. In the face of this " mur d'argent " Flandin had to accept a compromise, satisfactory to nobody; the Bank agreed to accept short-term bonds as collateral for loans at one-eighth of one per cent higher interest than the regular discount rate.[18] Annoyed with this " penalty rate," most banks and private investors (who doubtless shared the Bank's opposition to " reflation ") remained unconvinced of the desirability of increasing their portfolios of government securities.

The impasse was finally resolved by the rapid and disastrous repercussions on the French financial world of the Belgian devaluation of March, 1935. Speculators started a new attack on the franc, gambling that the near future would bring a French devaluation. The gold exodus from France began to assume alarming proportions. Between May 20 and May 24 alone the reserves of the Bank of France dropped by more than 1.5 billion francs.[19] Communist successes in the May municipal elections indicated a political trend that further agitated the money-market. In June the government of Flandin fell after an unsuccessful bid for financial plenary powers; a new government under Buisson lasted only a few days, and on June 7, 1935 Pierre Laval became president of the French Council of Ministers. Deflation was to be given another and more sweeping trial.

The Laval decree-laws.—The Bank of France immediately showed itself quite willing to lend substantial aid to the new administration. In return the government promised to take all measures necessary to balance the budget. The legislature then granted the new government plenary powers: " In order to

18 Wynne, *op. cit.*, p. 502. The Bank in return exacted a promise from the government that only 2.5 billion francs in new securities would be issued.

19 Germain-Martin, *op. cit.*, p. 305.

avoid monetary devaluation, the Senate and the Chamber of
Deputies give the government authorization until October 31,
1935 to enact by decree having the force of law [all measures]
to fight against speculation and to defend the franc." [20]

The new phase of deliberate deflation began with a vengeance. From July until October, 1935 the Laval government
issued a grand total of 549 " decree-laws." Almost no sector
of the French economy and administration was untouched. The
first and most important groups of deflationary decrees, issued
in July, slashed a flat 10 per cent from almost every wage and
price under the control of the government. All governmental
administrative budgets were cut 10 per cent, except those for
national security and for relief of unemployment. Employees
of local governments suffered the same salary reductions as the
national functionaries; those employed in colonies, on the
State's railroad system, and in subsidized concerns such as the
merchant marine did not escape. The price of bread was
ordered cut by 10 per cent, and also the price of all utilities
and of all rents, public and private. The *rentiers* were not
spared: interest on government bonds was subjected to a 10
per cent reduction.

The second group of deflationary measures undertaken by
Laval came in August, 1935. They ordered a general tighten-
ing up of all government bureaus in the interest of efficiency
and economy. In October the third and last group of Laval
decree-laws was introduced, this time with the objective of
unifying the administrative bookkeeping system, also in the
interest of efficiency.

The money-market and the public debt.—The champions of
deflation had regarded the growth of the public debt as their
private dragon. The Bank of France, for example, took the
position that the weakness of the franc and the flight of capital
were the result of the despair which seized all who contem-

20 *JO, Lois et Décrets*, June, 1935, p. 6298. For an exposé of the government's motives in asking for " pleins-pouvoirs," see *JO, Débats, Chambre,*
1935, p. 1810.

plated the ever-increasing burden of national indebtedness.[21]
All the efforts of the deflationary administrations had not been
able to reduce governmental expenditures below fifty billion
francs for 1935; this was five billion francs less than the sum
for 1933, but still six billions higher than that for the prosperity year 1928. By the end of 1935 the public debt had risen
to 338 billion francs, an increase of 64 billions since 1931. The
heart of the stoutest budget-trimmer quailed before the realization that 40 per cent of all expenditures went to service the
national debt, and another 20 per cent was taken up by military
expenses and pensions.[22]

At first little difficulty had been experienced in floating issues
of long-term bonds to meet the budgetary deficits. In September, 1932, in fact, the Treasury's position was still so strong
that the 5, 6, and 7 per cent *rentes* (of which 85 billion francs
were outstanding in that month) were successfully converted
to 4.5 per cent *rentes; the rentiers* grumbled, but most of them
took the new and less remunerative securities.

The Treasury was much less successful in its efforts to promote the sale of short-term obligations. As fiscal difficulties
mounted and the international situation grew more menacing,
the money-market fought shy of the once-desired *bons de la
défense nationale*. Interest rates on the *bons de la défense nationale* rose from 2.75 to 4.0 during 1933.[23] The public did not
have enough confidence in the monetary situation to accept the
lower interest rates usually offered by the short-term securities.

As the Treasury met continued revenue deficits with more
and more appeals to the money-market, general uneasiness over
the fiscal situation drove long-term interest rates up, to the
point where in January, 1935 the Treasury found it necessary

21 *Ibid.*, p. 311.

22 In the United States in 1935 less than 12 per cent of total expenditures
went to pay the interest on the public debt.

23 *La France économique en 1933*, p. 579.

to reassure the public that all possible efforts would be taken to balance the budget before any further long-term loans were floated. The average rate of interest on governmental long-term securities rose from 3.84 per cent in 1932 to 4.14 in 1934. In 1935 the long-term interest rate fell again, to 3.88 per cent; but similar interest rates in the United States and Great Britain had fallen below 3.00 per cent by that year.[24] Meanwhile interest rates on call loans (*argent à vue*), reflecting the slump in business conditions, fell away to almost nothing.

The efforts of the Bank of France to halt the gold " hemorrhage " by raising the discount rate only resulted in increased tension in the Parisian money-market. In May, 1935, shortly after the Belgian devaluation, the discount rate shot up from 2.5 to 6 per cent; as an expression of confidence in the Laval administration, it was lowered to 3 per cent in August, but by the end of 1935 it was up to 6 per cent again.[25] Between May, 1935 and May, 1936 the Bank changed its discount rate fifteen times.[26]

The distressed Treasury found that now that it was committed to avoiding recourse to *rentes,* little help could be expected from short-term Treasury bonds, its other main instrument of borrowing. One month after the Belgian devaluation, the value of *bons du Trésor* outstanding was reduced by 1.2 billion francs.[27] The desperate authorities again turned to the Bank of France for help: the Bank was asked to bolster the market for *bons* by agreeing to discount them in unlimited quantities. Until the Laval administration the Bank had steadfastly refused similar requests, arguing that only if the budget were balanced would pressure on *bons* disappear. But Laval persuaded the administrators of the Bank to agree to discount at regular rates *bons du Trésor* which the government sold to

24 Wormser, *op. cit.,* pp. 91-92.

25 *L'Evolution de l'économie française,* Table 45.

26 *La France économique en 1935,* p. 686.

27 Germain-Martin, *op. cit.,* pp. 306-307.

private banks. The *Caisse des dépôts et consignations* also
agreed to help out by investing in an additional amount of
bons.[28] These agreements paved the way for 13.8 billion francs
in indirect loans from the Bank through the medium of *bons
du Trésor,* or about three-quarters of the total value of such
bons outstanding in June, 1936.[29] The Treasury felt that this
" detour " was preferable to direct advances from the Bank,
in view of the country's deep-seated prejudices against the
latter form of borrowing.

One result of these face-saving advances was that the currency contraction which would have resulted from the capital
flight of perhaps sixteen billion francs in 1935 was in part neutralized. In satisfying its obligations, the Treasury fed into the
economy the currency received for its *bons* from the Bank of
France. Note circulation therefore remained stable at about
eighty-two billion francs in 1935 and the first few months of
1936. The monetary shrinkage which did occur took the form
of a decline in bank deposits. During 1935 deposits at the Bank
of France fell from sixteen to nine billion francs. Over the
same period, however, deposits at the " Big Four " and at
twenty-one important private banks declined only slightly
(from thirty to twenty-seven billions, and from seventeen to
fifteen billion francs, respectively), while deposits at the savings banks rose slightly during 1935 to a total of sixty billion
francs.

In October, 1935 the grant of financial plenary powers to
the Laval government came to an end. Laval did not ask for
another chance. All of the hundreds of deflationist measures
since the summer of 1932 had involved only 16.2 billion francs
of budgeting economies on paper. Actually, the net savings
achieved by these measures probably amounted to less than
that figure.[30] Budgetary deficits continued to accumulate; the

28 *Ibid.,* p. 321.

29 *Ibid.,* p. 323, and P.-B. Vigreux, *De la monnaie à l'économie en France
(1933-1938)* (Paris: Librairie générale de droit et de jurisprudence, 1938),
p. 132.

30 Wormser, *op. cit.,* p. 53.

public debt continued to grow. The whole complicated campaign of price deflation was brought to nought by the rise of French wholesale and retail prices in the fall of 1935. Meanwhile, the high exchange value of the franc continued to choke off French exports. The experiments in deliberate deflation were abandoned with few regrets.

Those in favor of a devaluation as the way out now became much more vocal. But the Sarraut government, which followed that of Laval, refused to take the dreaded plunge. Municipal elections in the spring of 1935 had seemed to indicate that the 1936 national elections would result in a victory for the parties of the Left. The moderate parties in control of the Fifteenth Legislature, therefore, simply marked time on monetary and fiscal questions, realizing that the onus of devaluation, if it came to pass, would have to be borne by their political opponents.[31]

DEPRESSION AND STAGNATION

A study of the vicissitudes of the French economy from 1932 until the beginning of the Second World War presents one of the most discouraging aspects of France's inter-war history. Neither the world-wide recovery from depression, nor the Popular Front " reflationist " experience, nor the preparations for another war seemed to have any lasting effect on the depressed level of French industrial production. Here we have one of the main facets of the much-discussed French weakness in the face of the Nazi challenge. Whether industrial weakness was cause or result of other (political, financial, social, or " moral ") disturbances in France is a most complicated problem. But whatever the sequence of causality involved, in 1939 French industry, producing at a rate barely equal to that of 1913, had to face a highly-developed and expanded German industrial complex which had been completely geared to the needs of total war.

31 Wolff, *op. cit.*, pp. 191-192.

Production and income during the depression.—The peak of French industrial production in the inter-war decades was reached in February, 1930, at an index of 112.6 (1928 = 100).[32] During the rest of 1930 the decline of industrial activity was rather slow. But in 1931 the process of contraction was speeded up; a trough was reached in April, 1932, at an index of 75.6. In the fall of 1932 observers rejoiced in the appearance of industrial recovery. The general index of industrial production rose to 90.6 in June, 1933, but this was to prove another downward turning point rather than the end of the Great Depression. Slowly but inexorably industrial production shrank each month during the rest of 1933 and all of 1934. By April, 1935 the index of industrial production had reached a trough of 76.4, about the same level as that of the 1932 slump. By then the annual number of bankruptcies had increased to extremely serious proportions.[33]

While French industry remained in a state of almost unrelieved depression between 1932 and 1935, industry in other countries was beginning to recover. All other important industrial powers "touched bottom" in 1932 and thereafter raised their production each year, at least until 1937. Between 1929

GENERAL INDEXES OF INDUSTRIAL PRODUCTION [34]

(1929 = 100)

	United Kingdom	Germany	United States	Italy	France
1930	92.3	85.9	80.7	90.7	100.4
1931	83.8	67.6	68.1	77.5	88.9
1932	83.5	53.3	53.8	72.3	68.8
1933	88.2	60.7	63.9	82.9	76.7
1934	98.8	79.8	66.4	90.7	71.0
1935	105.7	94.0	75.6	96.4	67.4

32 This is a newer and better index of the *SGF* than that available for earlier periods, for which the base year was 1913.

33 H. A. Arndt, *The Economic Lessons of the Nineteen-Thirties* (London: Oxford University Press, 1944), p. 139.

34 League of Nations, *Production mondiale et les prix, 1936-1937* (Geneva, 1938), p. 49.

and 1931 France had exhibited a remarkable resistance to the world depression compared to other nations, but now conditions appeared to be reversed. All of the five great Western powers gained in industrial production during 1933; only France declined in 1934 and in 1935.

By 1935 all signs of business activity indicated that France was suffering one of the worst slumps in her recent history. The index of cotton textile production (1928 = 100) fell from 92.6 in April, 1934 to 66.2 one year later.[35] One-fourth of the cotton mills at Roubaix were bankrupt.[36] The index of building activity (1928 = 100) fell from 90 at the beginning of 1934 to 66 in the spring of 1935.[37] Good advice given to the industrialists to adopt more modern machinery went unheeded for the most part because of the absence of profit incentives and the uncertain social and political situation. By the end of the depression the efficiency of France's industrial equipment was even further behind her competitors than in 1929.

As the depression wore on it became evident that France would suffer a serious blight of unemployment in spite of her characteristically small-enterprise economy. Even the usual " safety-valve " of immigrant laborers proved to offer no immunity; in 1932, after hundreds of thousands of foreign workers had been forced to leave, France's unemployed on public relief rolls rose from negligible numbers to 274,000; by 1935 there were 426,000 *chomeurs secourus*.[38]

The picture was not so black for the worker who managed to keep his job. Neither depression nor deliberate deflation

---

35 NBER, 1,186.

36 *La France économique en 1934*, p. 824.

37 NBER, 2,76.

38 Nogaro, *op. cit.*, p. 82. Even including with this figure Nogaro's estimate of " frictional " unemployment (200,000 workers), unemployment in 1935 amounted to less than five per cent of France's total occupied population.

succeeded in reducing hourly or daily wage rates very considerably; the real wages of non-governmental workers in many industries tended to rise at this time. The salaries of governmental employees were cut by about 16 per cent by the deflationist governments between 1932 and 1935.[39] Over the same period the index of the cost of living fell by almost the same amount—17 per cent.[40]

For the nation as a whole, income was subjected to severe and unrelieved shrinkage during the depression years. National monetary income fell from 229 to 175 billion francs from 1931 to 1935.[41] Expressed in terms of stable (1938) prices, the decline in national income was much less: from 369 billion francs in 1931 to 324 billions in 1935.[42] If the drop in national income was not so great proportionately as that, say, of the United States, the downward trend was three wearisome years longer; and when the upturn in monetary income finally came in 1936, it was almost completely wiped away by the concurrent rise in prices.

Wholesale and retail price movements.—The decline in French business activity and income was accompanied by a continuous drop in French wholesale prices. The still-born recovery of 1933 was marked by a levelling out of wholesale prices near an index of 400, but in the spring of 1934 the downward movement was resumed. From January, 1934 until July, 1935 the general index of wholesale prices dropped from 405 to 322.[43]

39 *Inventaire*, p. 348.

40 This was a new and improved index of the cost of living, calculated by the *SGF* for each *département* and averaged for all France, with 1930 as a base year. The older index had 1914 as a base year and applied only to Paris and a few other cities. Both indexes were based on the needs of " a working-class family of four."

41 Estimates of Dugé de Bernonville.

42 Estimates of Froment and Gavanier.

43 *SGF*: 126 articles, 1913 = 100.

During most of 1934 and 1935 the wholesale price index of foodstuffs was falling rapidly, but this drop was hardly attributable to the deflationary edicts. French authorities who worked in general for lower prices exempted foods from price cutting. Although this meant a higher cost of living, higher wages, and higher costs of production for French industry, the contradiction was forced on the deflationist governments by the realities of national political life.[44] The downward trend of food prices, therefore, was in *spite* of government policy, which, far from being directed toward cutting agricultural prices, had resulted in building up an almost impenetrable protectionist wall for France's farmers. But even in this " closed system " the prices commanded by French foods fell faster in 1934 and 1935 than at any other time during the Great Depression.

The end of the price recession in French agriculture came just at the time (July, 1935) when Laval was beginning the last and most vigorous attempt to cut budgetary expenditures and the cost of production in France. Since retail prices and the cost of living were closely bound up with the cost of food, the rise of wholesale prices doomed Laval's efforts before they were well under way.

The other component of the French wholesale price index, the index of industrial products and raw materials, had an entirely different history from that of foodstuffs in this period. In the summer of 1932 the industrial products index reached a low point where it remained, with very little change, while food prices continued to fall. At the end of 1934 the foodstuffs index fell below the industrial products index for the first time since 1930.

44 The French peasant is the perennial darling of the legislature. Peasant origins—and even peasant mannerisms—were considered great assets by French aspirants for political office. City families with dwindling incomes were appeased to a slight extent by the 10 per cent cut in the price of bread.

The comparative stability of the industrial materials index is another indication of the failure of the policy of deflation, since these obviously were prices which had to fall if French

CHART 5.   PRICE MOVEMENTS DURING THE DEPRESSION

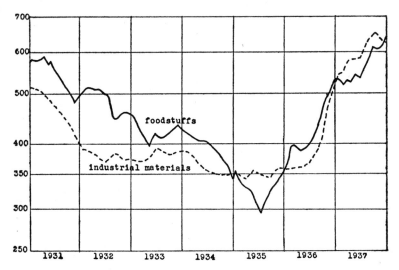

SOURCE: *SGF*. Components of the General Index of Wholesale Prices of 126 Articles. 1913 = 100.

exports could begin to sell at competitive prices without a devaluation of the franc. The resistance of the prices of industrial materials to deflation was partly a function of the French tariff policy. Many of these products were imported from the sterling or dollar areas, and a drop in this index could have been expected as a result of the British and American devaluations in 1931 and 1934. The drop in 1931 did appear, but by the time the dollar was devalued, the quota system was extended to protect French industry in addition to French agriculture, and the result was extremely " sticky " wholesale industrial prices.

Once France was closed off by protectionism, the compressibility of food prices proved greater than that of industrial prices, since the millions of French farmers were unable to control their total output. The crop yields of 1934 were exceptionally good; being perishable, a larger volume of foodstuffs had to be placed at the disposal of consumers just at a time when the French national income was at one of the lowest points in its recent history. A continued drop in food prices was the result.

France was the last of the great industrialized nations to see an upward turn in the general index of wholesale prices. The United States reached a turning point in wholesale prices in February, 1933; Great Britain in March, 1933; Germany in April, 1933; and Italy in July, 1934.[45] A similar upward turning point for France was not reached until July, 1935.

Retail prices and the cost of living in France also continued to fall after they had recovered in other countries. The index of retail prices in France reached a trough only in August, 1935. The cost of living in the United States, Germany, and Great Britain began to increase in April, 1933, two years before the cost of living in France ended its decline.[46]

Balances of payments.—The contraction of national income by the deflationary measures of the French authorities obviously contributed to the prolongation of the French business depression. But another important factor was the growing paralysis of France's foreign trade. The more the domestic economy of France suffered from the depression, the more important were her foreign markets; but French exports constantly deteriorated because of the world depression, the trend toward protectionism, and (thanks partly to the misguided efforts of the deflationary governments) the continued overvaluation of the franc.

The export and maritime industries had been hit first in the French depression, before those producing for the domestic market reacted to the world crisis. French commodity exports

45 League of Nations, *Revue de la situation économique mondiale, 1934-1935* (Geneva, 1936), p. 48.

46 *Ibid.*, p. 57.

did not even benefit from the short-lived recovery of 1933. The total value of exports shrank from 42.8 billion francs in 1930 to 30.4 in 1931 and 19.7 in 1932. Thereafter the decline was slower, reaching a trough of 15.5 billion francs in 1935. The decline in volume of exports, as distinguished from value, was less spectacular but hardly less inexorable.[47]

As drastic as was this decline of commodity exports, imports fell at an even faster rate, so that France's deficit in the balance of trade was reduced from ten billion francs in 1932 to six billions in 1935. Manufactured articles and foods were increasingly shunted away from France by more stringent tariffs and quotas. Contemporary observers gained what small comfort they could from this decreased unfavorable balance of trade.[48]

Because of the smaller unfavorable balance of trade, the deficit in the balance of current payments[49] was smaller in 1935 than in 1932.[50] Tourist items did continue to fall, however; as the franc became ever more dear in terms of foreign currencies, travellers began to pass by France for countries where their money would go farther. During 1935 the tourist trade in France was reduced to a humiliating position: Frenchmen travelling abroad spent just about as much money as did foreigners in France.[51] The government even considered the establishment of a "tourist franc" to overcome the obstacle to travel in France presented by the relative dearness of the

47 The quantum index of exports (1927 = 100) fell from 89.7 in 1930 to 54.2 in 1935; the trough, however, was in 1936 at an index of 51.2.

48 L'Institut de statistique de l'université de Paris and L'Institut scientifique de Recherches économiques et sociales, *L'Activité économique*, 1935 (Paris: Recueil Sirey, 1935), p. 8. (Hereinafter referred to as "*L'Activité économique*," with the appropriate year.)

49 For France and her empire (not including Indo-China).

50 For the period 1932-1935, the total current deficit was 9.7 billion francs; "reverse multiplier" effects must have reduced national income by much more than this sum.

51 *La France économique en 1935*, p. 632.

franc on foreign exchanges.[52] It is estimated that in 1935 tourist expenditures in France were only 750 million francs, compared to about eight billions annually between 1926 and 1931 and 2.5 billions even as late as 1934.[53]

The dearth of foreign markets came in part from factors over which France had little control. The depression not only shrank the total of world trade but also unleashed vigorous movements abroad for the protection of domestic industry. In 1932 the abandonment of free trade by the British hurt France's important trade with that country; the devaluation of the pound in 1931, furthermore, gave the whole sterling area an advantage over France in the " race for cheap money." The French tariff and quota system was to some extent a defensive move against the increased competition from British goods. But on the whole the exports of France and other gold standard countries to Britain were checked, while imports remained relatively high.

	Percentage, Total U. K. Imports from Gold Standard Countries	Percentage, U. K. Exports to Gold Standard Countries [54]
1930–1931	28.15	22.0
1932–1934	15.0	20.1

The devaluation of the dollar further aggravated the over-valued position of the franc. Between April, 1933 and April, 1934 the franc rose from 3.9 to 6.6 cents, making the dollar about 40 per cent cheaper in terms of francs. Now the dollar area, in addition to the sterling bloc, possessed a monetary unit relatively cheap in terms of the currency of gold bloc countries. About 40 per cent of France's former customers now enjoyed a trade advantage in the form of undervalued currencies. The dollar remained steady until the 1936 devaluation of the franc,

52 *Ibid.*, p. 823. In January, 1948 the French government did establish a " free " and very advantageous exchange rate for tourists from " hard money " countries.

53 *L'Evolution de l'économie française*, Table 19.

54 Seymour Harris, *Exchange Depreciation* (Cambridge: Harvard University Press, 1936), p. 442.

but the pound sterling continued to drop. Before September, 1931 the pound had been worth 124.21 francs. In 1932 and 1933 it fluctuated between 80 and 95 francs. During 1934 it fell again from 83 to 76 francs, and during most of 1935 it was worth a bit less than 75 francs.[55]

The drop in French prices could not begin to make French goods cheap enough to compete successfully in foreign markets. In 1930, for example, a French automobile selling for 20,000 francs cost a foreign buyer the equivalent of 161 pounds sterling. But at the lowered rate of 75 francs per pound, a similar auto cost 266 pounds in 1935. Even arguing that the price of the same auto might have fallen to 16,000 francs, it would still cost the foreign buyer 213 pounds sterling.[56]

More disturbing to many Frenchmen than either the low volume of trade or the slump in national income was the drain of gold out of the country. Public officials, bankers, economists, entrepreneurs—all cherished an apparently unshakable belief in the gold standard. One of the most important aspects of their faith was the principle that the more gold in a country, the better that country could resist " attacks " on its financial system. To them the inflow of gold from 1927 to 1932 was an expression of France's strength in the economic world; they could only interpret the exodus of precious metal after 1932 as a prelude to disaster.

The high tide of the flow of gold into France was reached in the fall of 1932, when the reserves at the Bank of France amounted to more than eighty-three billion francs. In the previous three years the Bank's gold reserves had doubled. In 1931 and 1932 the loss of gold which would have been brought about

55 Compiled from the *Revue d'économie politique.* The British Exchange Equalisation Account forced sterling down in order to keep it from appreciating in terms of the devalued dollar.

56 Nogaro, *op. cit.*, p. 268. Using cost of living indexes and a base period of September, 1931, the *Economist* (May 30, 1936, p. 492) calculates that at the end of 1935 the franc was overvalued 26 per cent in relation to the pound sterling and 33 per cent in relation to the dollar.

by the deficit on current account was more than counterbalanced by the flow of capital to France. During 1933 this tendency was checked; the export of gold from France just about balanced its import, and the reserves at the Bank of France fell off slightly toward the end of the year to about seventy-seven billion francs.

Settled financial conditions in Great Britain and the United States after the devaluations in those countries now began to reduce the comparative attractiveness of France as a haven for liquid capital. The relative confidence in the London, New York, and Paris money-markets was abruptly changed in the beginning of 1934, moreover, by the serious political situation in France. The riots of February, 1934 caused extreme uneasiness in the financial world; during the week ending February 9 alone the Bank of France's gold reserves dropped by two billion francs.[57] The obvious failure of the deflationary expedients of Doumergue, the budgetary crises of 1934-1935, and the devaluation of the belga all added to the anxiety of the once-bitten, devaluation-shy French owners of liquid capital. The total net loss of gold reserves at the central bank was sixteen billion francs in 1935; the total outward movement of gold from France was fifteen billion francs.[58] Almost all of the latter sum represented losses due to an outflow of " hot money " since the loss from a deficit on current account was reduced to less than one billion francs in 1935.

Commenting on the future of the gold standard at this time, Gustav Cassel pointed out that the whole foundation of the gold

57 *Le Temps financier*, February 19, 1934. One observer estimated the total flight of capital during this crisis at eight or nine billion francs. *La France économique en 1934*, p. 678.

58 The difference represents hoarding and " earmarking " operations. After the devaluation of the dollar the American authorities were reluctant to exchange gold for currencies divorced from gold (as was the pound at this time). The British Exchange Equalisation Account thereupon began to use francs and the facilities of the Bank of France in operations designed to keep the pound steady by buying or selling gold and foreign exchange.

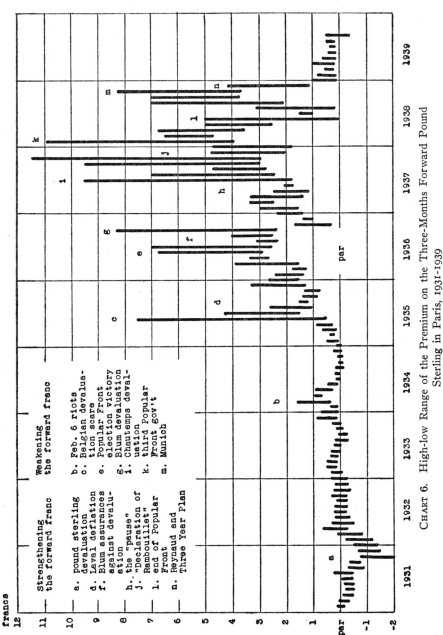

CHART 6.   High-low Range of the Premium on the Three-Months Forward Pound
Sterling in Paris, 1931–1939

SOURCE: Bank of France, *Cours des changes* (Unpublished records).

bloc was the continued inviolability of the French franc. " In this respect," said Cassel, " the gold bloc is an extremely weak construction." [59] By the beginning of 1936 most financiers and economists outside of France were agreed that the franc must soon be forced off gold.

In the spring of 1935 the weakness of the franc in the international exchange was demonstrated when the " forward " pound and dollar rates in Paris abruptly and dramatically shot up to substantial premiums. Aside from the crisis at the time of the February riots in 1934, the three-months forward pound had been selling close to par, or, as during the City panic in 1931, at a discount. The dollar also had been exhibiting " weakness" relative to the franc on the forward exchange. Now, as a consequence of the Belgian devaluation and the expected end of the gold bloc, the premium on the forward pound shot up from less than one franc in April, 1935 to 7.50 francs in May. The deflationary drive of the Laval régime had the effect of bringing this premium down to just under one franc by September of 1935; but with the abandonment of deflation the forward exchange turned against the franc, reaching a premium of 7.00 francs per pound sterling when the Popular Front took office. The speculators' money was placed on an inevitable devaluation of the franc.

WHY DEFLATION?

It has become fashionable, especially since the " Keynesian Revolution," to heap scorn upon the heads of those who formulated French monetary policy during the early 1930's. For those who wish to see their own countries spared similar abortive responses to similar circumstances, it is important to understand the patterns of thought which gave rise to such a policy.

Even the United States and Great Britain instinctively fell back on deliberate deflation, at least at the first onslaught of

59 *Op. cit.*, p. 204.

the depression.[60] Switzerland and Holland—other members of the gold bloc—experienced the bitterly frustrating results of deliberate deflation. Poland's deflationary policies were even more fatally " successful " than those of France; her efforts to stay on the gold standard and to resist devaluation created conditions of economic crisis which in 1935 gave her a more depressed index of industrial production than any other country publishing such an index.[61]

To the French it seemed that prudence and logic were all on the side of the advocates of budgetary equilibrium and deflation. The alternative offered by the significantly few proponents of devaluation [62] was a dangerous voyage on uncharted seas.

The French authorities were as much concerned as any with the well-being of their country. But for one reason or another their eyes were fixed narrowly on monetary and financial difficulties rather than the economic bases of these difficulties. This explains the overriding preoccupation with balancing the budget, defending the gold standard, and " protecting the patrimony of the thrifty " *rentiers*.

One of the main factors which forced the State back on a policy of cutting expenditures is to be found in the organization and policies of the chief French financial institution. Originally established as a private institution issuing bank-notes in return for deposits and promissory notes, the Bank of France had always been extremely reluctant to grant advances to the State. The Bank's traditional position was that these advances represented direct and inflationary additions to purchasing power, while bank-notes issued upon discounting commercial notes or accepting deposits represented the real monetary needs of the business community. The reconstruction effort after the

60 Hodson, *op. cit.*, p. 363.

61 League of Nations, *La Production mondiale et les prix, 1936-1937* (Geneva, 1937), p. 49. See also Cassel, *op. cit.*, p. 195.

62 The outstanding exceptions were Paul Reynaud and, interestingly enough, Marcel Déat. *JO, Débats, Chambre,* 1935, pp. 2240-2243.

First World War had forced the government to borrow heavily from the Bank, and a close correlation developed between Bank-to-State advances and bank-notes in circulation, especially between 1924 and 1927.[63] During the financial crises of 1925 and 1926 the " financially hypersensitive " French learned to interpret an increase in the column " avances extraordinaires à l'Etat " in the weekly Bank of France report as a step nearer to disaster. Even when the State was borrowing most heavily from the Bank, as in 1925, the legislature insisted on making at least token gestures toward repayment of these debts. One of the most popular financial measures of the Poincaré government was its repayment of all these " extraordinary " loans during 1927 and 1928.

To meet the fiscal needs of the country when tax receipts began to drop during the depression, therefore, the French government did not dare to turn to advances. The Treasury was forced to float an increasingly large number of bonds to meet the budgetary deficits. The public debt rose, and the government was saddled with a debt service which steadily became more burdensome not only in terms of absolute size [64] but also because of the increased value of the French monetary unit resulting from the price decline during these years.

The only answer the champions of budgetary deflation could give to this unfortunate state of financial affairs was to renew their demands for a reduction of the public debt, to be accomplished by lowering State expenditures and increasing taxes. Such was the power of the traditional fear of " monetary manipulations" by the State.

Several of the considerations which made for a policy of budgetary deflation were mainly political in nature. Because of the powerful political position of the French *rentiers,* most French politicians during this period had a blind spot concerning devaluation, which, with outright "bankruptcy," was re-

63 See Chapter II.

64 Advances from the Bank would not have carried interest charges.

garded as the alternative to deflation. The devaluation of 1928 had cost the *rentiers* four-fifths of the value of their bonds, it was argued. None of the French parties was interested in political suicide; the Popular Front government, right up until September, 1936, steadfastly denied any intention of further reducing the exchange value of the franc. French politicians between 1933 and 1936 were more concerned with protecting the purchasing power of their constituents' investments than with correcting the strangulating effect of the overvalued franc.

A most important group of factors behind the French policy of deliberate deflation was the body of attitudes and doctrines approved by contemporary French financial circles. For lack of a better name, we may consider them as " psychological " factors. Chief among these was the stubborn defense of the gold standard as the " condition of a return to normal trade and to production in conformity with the needs and possibilities of each country." [65] French business and political leaders were proud of the " strength " of France indicated by the great quantity of gold which had entered the country between 1926 and 1932. The prosperity of France during these years came to be identified with this reservoir of gold, and its very existence made it apparent that France could not be forced off a gold standard simply because of lack of sufficient gold.[66] Even after the exodus of gold in 1935, the value of gold reserves at the Bank of France was 64 per cent of the total value of bank-notes in circulation and deposits, well above the 35 per cent minimum established by the law of June, 1928.

Another " psychological " component of French deflationist policy was the unabated search for budgetary equilibrium, that Holy Grail of French inter-war financial history. The slogan of a balanced budget, with its easily-grasped implied analogy to the balance-sheet of a private enterprise, was a catch-all which substituted for a more sophisticated fiscal program.

65 *La France économique en 1933*, p. 482. Statement by Charles Rist.
66 See *Le Temps financier*, April 24, 1933.

Weakness in the theory and practice of deliberate deflation.
—The French policy of deflation, as it appeared in theory and practice, was anything but a complete and well-integrated program of economic and financial action. The fiscal and financial measures instituted by the deflationist governments were themselves full of contradictions. While an announced deflationist aim was to drive down French price levels, for example, certain French goods (especially foodstuffs) were protected by tariffs and quota systems. The merchant marine continued to receive its subsidies. Interest rates were raised by the central bank's attempts to check the outflow of gold through a rise in the discount rate. In 1935, during the most frantic stage of deflation, Laval was inflating the volume of currency in circulation by indirect advances from the Bank of France.

The weaknesses of the theories known as deflationist were just as glaring as the contradictions involved in deflationist practices. The most apparent of these lay in the superimposition of voluntary deflation on the deflationary conditions already existing as a result of the depression in France. In a complicated mechanism like the French State of the 1930's, with manifold and increasing responsibilities, there was no hope that national expenditures could be reduced enough to offset the decline in tax revenues caused by a severe depression. In the second place, the capitalist system is constituted so that entrepreneurial expansion usually can take place only with the prospect of greater profits. To provide these greater profits the advocates of deliberate deflation proposed to drive down wages, the cost of living, and interest rates so as to lower costs of production. But the fact that profit expectations thrive in an atmosphere of rising prices, not falling prices, had already been demonstrated by the business cycle studies of the 1920's. The inevitable effect of budgetary and cost deflation was to lower national income, whereas France's most pressing need after 1933 was to raise national income and investment. In so far as they were effective, therefore, the deflationist measures in

France only tended to aggravate the already existing depression.

The arguments for aligning the exchange rate of the franc through cost deflation were also open to criticism. The franc was overvalued in terms of dollars and pounds not only because prices inside the United States and Great Britain had fallen, but also because those countries had devalued their monetary units in terms of gold. Therefore, for France in the period 1933-1935 to have been able to recapture her favorable exchange position of 1928 through cost deflation, price levels in France would have had to be reduced approximately 35 per cent *from their already depressed levels*. Even granted that this tremendous deflation could have been accomplished rapidly and uniformly in regard to the many different price levels, it is difficult to imagine how the French economy could have withstood such a depressive shock.

From another point of view, the policy of voluntary deflation also entails severe injustices as it works itself out through the economy. The possessor classes—the *rentiers*—stand to gain from the increased purchasing power of the interest on their bonds. But the debtor classes suffer. Those taxpayers who supply the funds which are turned over to the holders of government bonds must bear the increasingly heavy burden of the debt service. And the economic depression accompanying falling prices may deprive the businessman of his profits and the worker of his job.

Our study of the period of deliberate deflation shows, furthermore, that the policy of deflation was not based on a rational and integrated body of theory, but developed out of the frantic attempts of the French government to solve the problem of budgetary deficits. To cut expenditures and raise taxes when faced with insufficient tax receipts was simply an instinctive reaction on the part of men who believed that the fiscal affairs of a nation were only a gigantic counterpart of the profit-and-loss situation of a private enterprise. The proposals to combat the depression and to correct the overvaluation of the franc through cost deflation were later developments—almost afterthoughts.

The severest criticism of all, of course, is that the experiments in deflation failed. They failed to achieve their primary aim of balancing the budget. The vicious cycle of deflation engendered by the addition of deliberate deflation to economic depression lowered tax returns while the needs of the government for funds increased. Business conditions were hurt, not helped, by deliberate deflation. The franc remained overvalued, to the great distress of the export and tourist trades. The inevitable reaction to this series of failures was the " reflationist " policies of the Popular Front.

CHAPTER V
POPULAR FRONT EXPERIMENTS

FROM LEFT TO RIGHT: THE MONETARY POLICIES
OF THE POPULAR FRONT

THE legislative elections in the spring of 1936 resulted, as expected, in an absolute majority in the Chamber of Deputies for the Popular Front. This combination of Communists, Socialists, and Radical-Socialists was modeled on the Spanish *frente popular;* it recognized " no enemies on the Left." The occasion for the appearance of Popular Front movements had been the about-face decision of the Communist Third International to cooperate with socialist and liberal elements everywhere in a struggle against the common enemy, fascism. But anti-fascism was only the negative aspect of this broad movement. Very definite social and economic aspirations were involved, which in France took the form of a group of policies designed, on the one hand, to improve the well-being of the " little people," and on the other, to end the long-drawn-out economic depression.

Development of Popular Front monetary policy.—The leaders of the new régime were concerned with so many vital economic, social, and political affairs that at first they paid scant attention to purely monetary and fiscal matters. They hoped that business recovery induced by reforms would automatically resolve France's budgetary difficulties. Blum and Auriol, his Minister of Finance, did not intend to dissipate their opportunities by becoming involved in the intricacies of the money-market. Unfortunately, the Popular Front's efforts did not produce a real revival of business activity; more and more the government was forced to devote its energies to narrowly monetary problems. Much against Blum's will, the life of his administration was finally tied to monetary stability; and it was during a financial crisis that his government was overthrown.

138

An examination of the monetary experiences of the Popular Front, therefore, is important for the understanding of this critical period in French history. But the subject is most complex. We have found it helpful to view the development of Popular Front monetary policy as a succession of three " phases." Not all of the events under discussion, of course, will fit into such an artificial grouping, but taken as a whole, each period is significantly different from the others. The first phase, during which business recovery was seen as a by-product of social reform, lasted until the franc was devalued (September, 1936); during the second phase (October, 1936 to February, 1937) the government hoped that devaluation would bring back émigré capital and allow a continuation of the reform program; the third phase, from February to June, 1937, saw the abandonment of further reforms in the interests of " confidence."

First phase—" reflation."—On June 5, 1936, two days after the formation of his new government, Blum outlined to the legislature what reflation was to mean in terms of new laws. First in the order of business was wiping out the distasteful remnants of deflation by annulling Laval's salary and pension cuts. Other " first series " economic measures included a project for paid holidays, an ambitious program of public works, and the establishment of a " Wheat Office " to set a minimum price for grains; this institution was intended to serve as a model for similar " offices " of wine and milk. Soon these" urgent and therefore limited " economic measures were supplemented by reduction of the work-week to forty hours (with no reduction of weekly salaries) and provisions for collective bargaining to help workers negotiate for higher salaries. In the enactment of these projects the Popular Front tried to implement its program of increased purchasing power by increasing salaries, pensions, and farmers' incomes through direct intervention by the government.

In the minds of the leaders of the Popular Front government, who were flourishing an urgent olive branch in the direction of the entrepreneurs, there was no conflict between the twin goals of reform and recovery. According to Premier Blum, improvement of the lot of the poorer classes was in the national interest. The new régime would, of course, fulfill its obligations to the workers: ". . . to absorb unemployment, to increase the mass of consumers' income, and to provide some well-being and security for all those who, by their labor, create real wealth. . ."; but at the same time it was through these very measures that the French national economy would be served. Raising wages and national purchasing power was not exclusively for the benefit of the workers; "reflation" would stimulate an increase in production and therefore lower per unit costs, since wages were a much less important fraction of costs than were fixed investments. Higher wages, therefore, meant higher profits.[1] This was certainly no policy of class conflict.

The government also took the position that there was no real reason why holders of liquid capital should fear the new economic and financial policies of the country. Auriol was most insistent that it was to the interest of owners of "hot money" and hoarded funds to stake their holdings on a revival of French business. Specifically, he said, they need have no fear of a devaluation of the franc.

Himself a former protagonist of devaluation, Auriol now argued that it was out of the question; it might lead to retaliatory devaluations of other monetary units and a situation which would degenerate into a race for cheap money.[2] In any case, he declared, devaluation would raise internal prices without any absolute guarantee of an improvement in foreign trade. Rather than attempting such an "adventure," Auriol continued, France should embark on a program of regaining confidence in her money; the estimated sixty billions of francs

1 *JO, Débats, Sénat,* 1936, pp. 493-496.

2 *JO, Débats, Chambre,* 1936, pp. 1500-1509. At the same time several former outstanding opponents of devaluation, including Germain-Martin and Charles Rist, were now in favor of devaluation. *Le Temps financier,* June 1 and June 8, 1936.

hoarded at home and abroad represented a much greater potential benefit to the national economy than any " monetary manipulations." He attacked in bitter terms those politicians and publicists who were frightening the people with baseless talk of "inevitable devaluation," and frankly admitted the government's need to stop the " gold hemorrhage." Finally, to discourage those " traitors to their country " who continued to falsify their statements of financial balances held abroad, Auriol proposed to increase punishments for fraudulent declarations and to make arrangements with foreign governments for disclosing the whereabouts of refugee French funds.

Changes in the administration of the Bank of France.—One of the most popular campaign pledges of the Popular Front had been to reform the Bank of France in order to make that " financial Bastille " more dependent on the State and less on private interests. The question of the political and economic power wielded by the " two hundred families " constituting the Bank's General Assembly had been a hotly debated issue.[3] In 1935 the *Confédération Générale du Travail* had begun a campaign to nationalize the Bank of France by expropriating its shares and repaying owners with government bonds.[4] A charge frequently made in the 1936 election campaign was that the Bank was using its secret funds (" caisse noire ") to influence voters against left-wing candidates.[5] But the Popular Front government rejected outright nationalization of the Bank of France, though some changes were made in the method of choosing its directing personnel.

Under the Bank's former charter, the two hundred chief stockholders, gathered in a " General Assembly," had elected a " Council of Regents " of fifteen plus three " censors " (aud-

3 Pirou, *La Monnaie française de 1936 à 1938* (Paris: Recueil Sirey, 1938), pp. 16-19.

4 A. Dumora, *La Réforme de la Banque de France et l'Evolution monétaire de juin 1936 à juin 1937* (Bordeaux: Imprimeries Delmas, 1939), p. 30.

5 Walter R. Sharp, *The Government of the French Republic* (New York: D. Van Nostrand Co., 1938), pp. 246-247.

itors); these eighteen, with the governor and two vice governors (appointed by the President of the Republic) were, in effect, the executive directorate of the Bank. According to the law of July 24, 1936,[6] the new General Assembly was to consist of *all* holders of Bank of France shares, each with one vote, rather than the two hundred holders of the largest blocks of shares.[7] The old Council of Regents was replaced by a new directing body of twenty-three members. While previously the General Assembly had elected all the members of the Bank's Council of Regents, the new " General Council " had only two members chosen by the shareholders. All the rest were chosen by the State. Nine were to represent the nation's " economic and social interests "—the chief labor organization (*Confédération Générale du Travail*), public savings banks, cooperatives, chambers of commerce, and chambers of agriculture. Nine were to be chosen from the " collective interests of the nation "— various governmental financial agencies including the *Crédit foncier,* the *Crédit national,* the *Caisse des dépôts et consignations,* and the Ministry of Finance itself. All the members of the new General Council were either chosen directly from the designated groups by the minister of finance or elected by the institution in question subject to his approval. The governor and the two vice governors of the central bank were, as in the past, chosen by the President of the Republic, and the three censors continued to be elected by the General Assembly.[8] With a rather subtle touch, Blum declared that the " Banque de France " might now be referred to as the " Banque de la France."

Such moderate reform of the Bank of France, like rejection of monetary devaluation, was in line with the government's policy of not discouraging financiers too much; their partici-

6 *JO, Lois et Décrets,* 1936, pp. 7810-7811.

7 In 1934 there were more than 40,000 investors owning Bank of France shares. Of these, nearly two-thirds held only one or two shares. Myers, *op. cit.,* p. 42.

8 Laufenburger, *op. cit.,* pp. 289-293.

pation was needed in national economic recovery. The French tax structure was changed only slightly; " a revivified economy will yield satisfactory revenues," declared Auriol. According to Léon Blum, ". . . the return to normal activity would resolve in itself the budgetary problem, since the deficit is not one of the causes of the depression but one of its results and one of its manifestations.[9]

The defeat of " reflation."—The success or failure of the Popular Front fiscal and economic experiments rested squarely on their ability to force an improvement in the long-stagnant French economy. This was the criterion demanded by the country and accepted by the government. From June until October, 1936 the Popular Front tried to implement its program of recovery through reform without the help of monetary devaluation. But the attempts of the government to promote business recovery failed unmistakably in almost every measurable sector of the economy. Not only was there little improvement in industrial production, for example, but the promising upward trend begun at the end of 1935 actually reversed itself.

The month of May, 1936 proved a downward turning point for most branches of industry; chemicals, textiles, and the leather trades were among the worst hit; at the same time a previous upward trend in mining and metal working was slowed down. The index of building trades activity, maintained at about 76 during the second half of 1935 and the first half of 1936 (1928=100), fell off in May and went as low as 60 in August, where it remained until the industry once again recovered after the devaluation of the franc.[10] Pig iron production fell from 538,000 metric tons in May, 1936 to 470,000 in June.[11] Cotton textile production reached an index of 93 in May (1928=100), fell to 85 in June, and was at the same level just before the devaluation.[12]

9 Broadcast speech at Narbonne, April 21, 1936.

10 NBER, 2,76.

11 *Ibid.*, 1,189.

12 *Ibid.*, 1,186.

For industry as a whole, the index of production dropped from 87.4 in May, 1936 to 75.5 in August. This trough was as deep as those of the worst months of 1932 and 1935. The uncertainties raised by Hitler's Rhineland *coup*, the Popular Front election victory, the " sit-down " strikes, and the newly enacted paid summer holidays all played a part in slowing down industrial activity. But after these events French industry still failed to achieve a recovery large enough to vindicate the Popular Front. In September the industrial production index stood at 81.2, no better than the same month in 1935.

Though the reduction in the length of the working week by the Popular Front government is generally blamed for many of France's misfortunes, this factor played no part in the industrial slump of the summer of 1936. Voted " in principle " on June 21, 1936, the forty-hour week law was not put into operation until November. The Matignon agreements of June 7, 1936, however, had succeeded in raising wages an average of 12 per cent. With the new law requiring paid vacations of two weeks, the increase in the cost of labor to entrepreneurs was roughly 16 per cent, *before* any widespread application of the forty-hour week.

From the point of view of the Communist and Socialist leaders of the Popular Front, the relief of unemployment in France was perhaps the most important goal of all, but the number of French workers unemployed remained undiminished in the second and third quarters of 1936 after falling off somewhat toward the end of 1935.[13] The index of unemployed on public relief rolls of the *SGF* (1926=100), which stood at 165 in June, 1936, rose each month thereafter until it reached 173 in September and stayed at that level in October.

Other aspects of French economic life were hardly more satisfactory. Assurances of the government against devaluation had halted temporarily the withdrawal of gold from the Bank of France; in September, however, a serious decline set in, and a low of fifty-two billion francs in gold was reached. This sum,

13 *L'Activité économique*, 1936, p. 199.

though still above the 35 per cent of the Bank's sight obligations required by law, was considered perilously close to a minimum war chest in such troublous times.[14] Meanwhile wholesale and retail prices, after remaining fairly steady in the first two quarters of 1936, had begun a precipitous rise in June, thereby aggravating the disparity between French and foreign prices and further weakening the already-moribund export and tourist industries. Continued stagnation, continued unemployment, and the appearance of a new " flight from the franc " forced the government to admit the defeat of its " reflationist " policies.

Second phase —" alignment."—It was under these circumstances that France undertook her second inter-bellum devaluation of the franc. Although this devaluation involved negotiations between France, Great Britain, and the United States over several months, it was a well-guarded secret. To the French, who for the most part had come to believe the government's repeated assurances that devaluation would not be forthcoming, it came as a complete surprise. The Communist party, one of the main supports of the Popular Front (though refusing to accept any ministerial positions), announced that it had learned about the devaluation at the same time as the rest of the country.[15] One of the Popular Front campaign slogans had been: " Neither deflation nor devaluation!" Premier Blum had declared himself opposed to a " coup d'état monétaire " and had asserted flatly that the 1928 gold parity of the franc would be maintained.[16]

There had been some hints, however, that the government's desire to avoid devaluation, while probably sincere enough, was not uncompromising. Auriol's pronouncements, for example, had emphasized the dangers of " retaliatory devaluations," implying that international assurances against a race

14 Pirou, *La Monnaie française de 1936 à 1938*, p. 31.

15 Jacques Duclos, *La Dévaluation* (Paris: Editions du comité populaire de propagande, 1936), p. 3.

16 Pirou, *La Monnaie française de 1936 à 1938*, p. 28.

for cheap money would permit a French devaluation.[17] In a speech to the Chamber of Deputies on June 16, 1936 Blum had admitted that while devaluation would help the budgetary problems of the State, it would do more harm than good unless protected by " international agreements and a general and contractual [monetary] alignment."

On September 26, 1936 the government suddenly announced that the obstacles to a devaluation of the franc had been met. In fact, on that day a declaration, the " Tripartite Monetary Pact," was released simultaneously in London, Paris, and Washington. " To safeguard peace, to favor the establishment of order in international relations, and to follow policies developing world prosperity and ameliorating the standard of living," this agreement stated, the United States and Great Britain " receive favorably " the news of the " adjustment " of France's monetary unit and promise that they will take steps to avoid difficulties in exchange markets as a result of the devaluation.[18] Other nations were invited to join in pledging to desist from attempts to secure " an advantage of exchange "; Belgium, Holland, and Switzerland added their signatures to the " Tripartite " agreement in November, 1936.

On October 1, 1936 the French franc's second devaluation in eight years was enacted into law. France abandoned the gold bullion standard established by Poincaré; the Bank of France was relieved of the obligation to redeem its notes in gold. The " aligned " franc, however, was still defined as a gold currency. It was to be fixed at some future date by decision of the Council of Ministers at a figure between forty-nine and forty-three milligrams of gold 900/1000 fine, instead of the 65.5 milligrams of the Poincaré franc. Because of its lack of a definite relationship to gold, the new " Auriol franc " was sometimes called the " elastic franc."

17 Vincent Auriol, *Un Bilan, un programme, des actes* (Paris: Librairie Populaire, 1936), p. 19.

18 Mehmet Mazhar, *La Dévaluation de la monnaie française de septembre, 1936 et les circonstances qui l'ont amenée* (Paris: F. Loviton et Cie., 1937), pp. 309-311.

The law of October 1, 1936 also provided for a revalorization of the central bank's gold reserves on the basis of forty-nine milligrams of gold per franc. Of the seventeen billion franc increase in the value of the Bank's holdings resulting from this revalorization, ten billions were used for the establishment of an Exchange Stabilization Fund, which, on the model of the British and American " Funds," was to keep exchange fluctuations of the new national monetary unit within fairly narrow limits. The remaining windfall profits from the revalorization of the gold reserves were turned over to the Bank of France to be applied against the advances which the Bank had granted the Treasury.[19]

Private holders of gold, according to the terms of this law, were not to benefit from the devaluation. They were given the choice of selling their precious metal to the Bank of France at the pre-devaluation rate or holding it by repaying the government a sum equal to the increase in the value of their holdings in terms of francs. Gold not declared could be confiscated. These provisions were criticized as forcing owners to hide their hoards instead of bringing gold back into the French economy, where it was needed; and in fact this law was neither obeyed nor enforced.

According to the terms of the new monetary law, the use of gold for international commercial transactions was dependent upon specific grants from the Bank of France for permission to buy its gold.[20] Shipment of gold abroad for the purpose of speculation was forbidden. Only the newly-established Exchange Stabilization Fund could export gold freely. But if speculators could not now obtain gold directly from the Bank of France, they could obtain other currencies which were redeemable in gold. In spite of severe criticism from the Communist party and from some Socialist and labor groups, the Popular Front government did not institute exchange control.

19 *La France économique en 1936*, p. 594.

20 Pirou, *La Monnaie française de 1936 à 1938*, p. 38. See also *Bulletin de Statistique et de législation comparée*, September, 1936, p. 528.

In explaining why the government did not seize control of the exchange market, Auriol pointed out that there were two solutions to the question of how to protect the gold war chest:

> . . . to lead the country into a régime of autarky by the incessant strengthening of protective tariffs, by exchange control, and by internal inflation; or rather to seek prosperity in a system of normal exchanges by the adjustment of our money to world prices and to other moneys. We have chosen this second solution, which is to say liberty.[21]

Emphasis on the need for gold and other liquid capital was characteristic of the monetary policy of the second phase of this Popular Front régime. The lack of adequate investment in French business was singled out as one of the main causes for the failure of the first Popular Front experiments.[22] At the same time one of the main goals of devaluation was to offer holders of capital additional inducement to bring their money into France by making the franc cheaper in terms of gold and foreign exchange.[23] Once refugee French funds and foreign capital began to find their way into France, it was hoped, interest rates would be lowered by the abundance of available capital, and this would open the way for a general economic revival.

Thus the monetary and economic policies of the second phase of the Popular Front represented an important change from those developed in the first five months. At first the government's hopes for recovery had been pinned on increases in mass purchasing power to be achieved by direct State intervention and by its indirect promotion of wage increases. Now that this method had proved a disappointment, the government shifted its hopes to imports of large amounts of privately-held liquid capital (to be induced by devaluation) as the motive force in bringing about revival of French business conditions.

21 *JO, Débats, Sénat*, 1936, p. 1415.

22 *JO, Débats, Chambre*, 1936, p. 2810.

23 Léon Blum, *L'Exercise du pouvoir* (Paris: Gallimar, 1937), p. 216.

Economic recovery still remained the basic consideration; as Blum declared, there was no real contradiction between the policies of the first and second phases of the Popular Front experiment. The premier announced that the new fiscal and economic program would simply ". . . seek the same objectives with different means." [24] And he pointed to changes in the " New Deal " of the United States as an example of courageous willingness to admit defeat and to strike out in a different direction.

According to Blum there had been three main reasons for the failure of the French economy to revive: (1) Hoarding and the continued lack of investment. Entrepreneurs remained " in a state of anxiety," partly for fear of international developments like the crisis caused by the Spanish civil war and the threatening military maneuvers of Hitler. (2) A new outbreak of important strikes in September. (3) The frightening rate of decrease in the Bank of France's gold reserves. The government was forced to choose between defending gold parity and defending its gold reserves.[25] In underlining the importance of mollifying capitalists and the patriotic necessity of protecting France's gold reserves, Blum implied that in the future the factor of " business confidence " would receive careful consideration. He appealed to the labor unions for " economic peace " and assured the Senate that the government had no intentions of instituting socialism in the national economy or authoritarian methods in the political sphere.[26]

In addition to incentives for a flow of capital to France, the devaluation carried with it the government's hopes for a stimulus to the depressed export and tourist trades. These important sectors of French economic life had suffered severely from the depression and from the discrepancy between French and

24 Ibid., pp. 222-223.

25 JO, Débats, Chambre, 1936, p. 2811.

26 Ibid., Sénat, 1936, p. 1430.

foreign price levels ever since the British and American devaluations. By lowering the exchange rate of the franc the government hoped to make French goods and services once more attractive to foreign importers and tourists.[27]

The Popular Front budgets.—The leaders of the Popular Front government were not concerned with balancing the budget as an end in itself. In view of the great rise in prices in 1936 and 1937, moreover, the budgetary deficits for those years were not much greater than for the preceding years, when great efforts had been made to achieve budgetary equilibrium. Part of the deficit of 1936 was attributable to a slump in tax receipts, and part to the outlay for public works and national defense in the first six months of the Blum régime. Arguing that the expenses of public works and national defense could not possibly be written off in one year, Auriol announced that the Treasury would limit its efforts at budgetary equilibrium to the " ordinary budget." The year 1936, therefore, saw the reappearance of an " extraordinary budget " for the first time since 1922. According to the administration, however, the extraordinary budget was more properly to be regarded as the " capital investment fund for the execution of the programs of national defense and of public works to stimulate economic recovery and to fight unemployment." [28]

In preparing the 1937 budget the Popular Front had to leave unbalanced even the *budget ordinaire*. There had not as yet been time enough for the social and economic reforms instituted by the Popular Front to take effect; therefore, the government announced, 1937 was to be regarded as a " year of transition." The " transitional " ordinary budget as passed was expected to have a deficit of 4.8 billion francs. The extraordinary budget, completely " in the red," was set at 20.3 bil-

27 The concept of " purchasing power parity " was invoked by the French at this time in deciding on the extent of their devaluation of the franc. See Heilperin, *op. cit.*, p. 136.

28 The 1936 fiscal year ended with a deficit of 16.9 billion current francs, 9.3 billions of which were attributable to the extraordinary budget.

lions, including 9.5 for national defense and 5.4 for public works.[29]

Effects of the 1936 devaluation on French business conditions.—In the months following the devaluation there was a moderate and rather qualified improvement in French business conditions. The export industries, especially, reflected the beneficial effects of the devaluation, while industrial production as a whole regained the position of the spring of 1936. The general index of industrial production rose to 93.4 in February, 1937, reaching the highest point attained since 1931.[30] The textile and chemical industries, automobile manufacturing, and pig iron made considerable gains. But industrial expansion was neither uniform nor spectacular. Mining, metallurgical industries, and the leather goods trades hardly showed the effects of recovery. And with the spring of 1937, the promise of a really important expansion of French industry faded. The last months of the Blum government were marked by another slump in industrial production.

A decline in the number of unemployed workers after the devaluation was one of the few bright spots in the rather gloomy picture. The index of " chomeurs secourus " (1926 = 100) fell from 173 in October, 1936 to 143 in April, 1937, where it remained until the business recession of 1938. But even this gain could not be attributed to the devaluation, since the forty-hour work week law was now being enforced in most large shops, offices, and factories. Worst of all, the sharp rise of retail and wholesale prices threatened to bring to nothing the achievements of the Popular Front in raising the income of the lower classes.

The hopes of the government for a substantial return of gold and capital to the French economy were realized only in part. The gold reserves at the Bank of France increased from sixty-two to sixty-four billion francs from September to November,

29 *La France économique en 1936*, p. 583. Actually, the retrenchment during the " pause " cut the total deficit for 1937 to 21.2 billion francs.

30 *SGF*, 1928 = 100.

1936, and then another slight decline set in; but since the establishment of the Exchange Stabilization Fund and its necessarily secret manipulations, the weekly report of the Bank of France could no longer be taken as an exact indication of the nation's gold reserves. There was a slight rise in commercial discounts at the Bank of France and in new stocks and bonds issued, indicating some increase in investment.

The second phase of the Popular Front régime thus failed either to provide much tangible improvement in French business conditions or to stimulate a significant inflow of capital. But the immediate factor which finally ended this phase was continued speculative pressure against the franc's exchange value as established in October, 1936. In spite of the operations of the Exchange Stabilization Fund, considerable discounts against the " forward " franc began to pile up immediately after the devaluation, necessitating large purchases of francs by the Fund in order to keep the " spot " exchange rate steady.

On January 29, 1937 the Stabilization Fund made the stunning announcement that the Auriol franc had been maintained at the October, 1936 level only at the expense of the Fund's entire gold allotment of ten billion francs. The Bank of France thereupon loaned the Fund another three billion francs in gold; but the Paris money-market became extremely pessimistic about the future of the franc, refusing to be reassured by a declaration by Auriol on February 5 that he was opposed to any further devaluation or to the establishment of exchange control.

Third phase—" pause."—Frightened by the specter of another collapse in the exchange rate of the franc, the government turned to a different set of financial and economic policies. On February 14, at a congress of the Socialist party, Blum announced a " pause " in social and economic reforms. In the future no further moves would be made which might undermine the confidence of the business community while the reforms already enacted were " digested."

During the next month a series of fiscal measures was advanced to implement the policy of the " pause." The government made some important cuts in expenditures, particularly by cancelling those projects for public works authorized but not yet actually begun, thus effecting a six billion franc reduction in the 1937 budget. Free trade in gold was reëstablished, with no penalties for those who had not declared their gold holdings as directed by the monetary law of October 1, 1936. Those who had obeyed the law and turned in their gold at the pre-1936 rate were recompensed.[31] A 4½ per cent loan was floated, payable either in French or in Swiss francs to guarantee it against exchange fluctuations. Blum reiterated his determination to uphold the Tripartite Monetary Pact and to maintain a free market in foreign exchange.

Bowing to the wishes of the financial community, the government appointed a " committee of experts " to manage the Stabilization Fund.[32] This committee abandoned the policy of maintaining the franc at a fixed relation to gold or to the pound sterling. At the beginning of April the franc was allowed to decline to an equivalent of 43 milligrams of gold, the lower limit set by the October monetary law.

The Paris money-market responded favorably at first to the new, more conservative policy of the government. The guaranteed loan was fairly successful, and the discount on " forward " francs declined again. But after only three months France suffered another speculative attack on the franc. The Stabilization Fund was hard pressed to keep the franc from falling lower. The sale of government securities was so unsatisfactory that the Treasury had to borrow 400 million francs from the *Caisse des dépôts et consignations* to meet its June bills.

Meanwhile French industry and commerce began another period of recession. The general index of industrial production (1928 = 100) fell from 93.6 in March, 1937 to 88.7 in June.

31 Pirou, *La Monnaie française de 1936 à 1938*, pp. 45-46.

32 Professors Rist, Baudouin, and Rueff of the University of Paris and Governor Labeyrie of the Bank of France.

Aside from the metallurgical and mechanical sectors of production, which were now responding to orders for armaments, the industrial slump was general.[33] Critics of Blum's economic policies saw more than a coincidence in the fact that this recession and the widespread application of the forty-hour week came at the same time. The recession appeared all the more serious when contrasted with the world-wide business recovery which was taking place in the spring of 1937. Tax receipts below expectations [34]—in spite of the steep price rise—and a drop in unit sales of the important department stores [35] showed that the new slump affected the whole business community.

The " pause " proved to be only a temporary check, furthermore, on the massive outflow of capital. The emigration of " hot money " was resumed in May, 1937, when it became obvious that the Exchange Stabilization Fund was again in difficulties. The more the government protested that it would not permit another devaluation, the more probable did devaluation appear to French speculators.

This émigré capital converged in a flood on London and New York. Monetary developments in England, especially, indicate the vastness of this movement of capital.[36] The British Exchange Equalisation Account, finding its sterling reserves exhausted by the inflowing funds, was forced to turn its surplus gold over to the Bank of England in exchange for pound notes. There was a perceptible rise in the note circulation of the Bank of England; it is estimated that at one time fifteen million pounds sterling were hoarded by citizens of France and other gold bloc countries.[37]

33 L'Activité économique, 1937, p. 13.

34 Ibid., p. 108.

35 Ibid., p. 123.

36 Some of these funds undoubtedly came from other gold-bloc countries, whose financiers expected a devaluation of their own currencies to follow that of the French franc.

37 Leonard Waight, The Exchange Equalisation Account (Cambridge: Cambridge University Press, 1939), p. 64.

While liquid capital was streaming out of France, the balance of payments on current account was taking a turn for the worse. During the " reflationary " period at the beginning of the Blum régime France imported a larger volume of goods, increasing the deficit in the balance of commodity trade. The beneficial effect of the September devaluation on the export industry lasted for only a few months. Because of the new labor laws, the rise in the cost of labor, and general distrust of the political situation, French industry was not in a good position to respond to the export inducement offered by the cheaper franc. Furthermore, some French exporters continued to charge the same amount of pounds or dollars for their wares, which of course meant greater profits in francs for them.[38] The unfavorable balance of commodity trade rose from six billion Poincaré francs in 1935 to 8.3 billions in 1936, and continued to rise in 1937.

With the less expensive franc there was some increase in tourist expenditures in 1936, though the amount was still insignificant compared to the level of tourist spending in the lush years between 1925 and 1931. Other " invisible export " items such as interest, dividends, and freight charges remained at their depressed 1935 level, at least when converted into francs of 1928 exchange value. As a result, the unfavorable balance of current payments rose from .8 billion Poincaré francs in 1935 to 2.9 billions in 1936 and continued to turn against France in 1937.

Between January and October, 1936 the adverse situations on both capital and current account resulted in an outflow of gold of about twenty-one billion Poincaré francs. After the devaluation there was a slight inflow, indicated by an increase in

38 *L'Activité économique*, 1937, pp. 218-219. This last maneuver was also evident after the French devaluation of January, 1948; French exporters of automobiles and liqueurs were denounced by the French press for not being satisfied with their old rate of profit; charging the same amount of foreign currency for exports deprived France of the competitive advantages to be gained from the devaluation in international trade.

the gold reserves of the Bank of France from 62.2 billion francs at the end of October to 64.3 at the end of November. But at the end of the year a decline appeared once again; by February, 1937, the Bank's gold reserves were down to 57.4 billions. At this point the announcement of the " pause " halted further declines until the panic of June, 1937 reduced the reserves to 50.2 billion Auriol francs. All told, the losses of the Bank of France's gold reserves during the Blum administration were about 14.6 billion Poincaré francs.

The panic of June, 1937.—The atmosphere of financial crisis in which the first Blum government was finally overthrown developed out of the dangerous position of the Treasury and an " attack " on the exchange rate of the franc. By mid-June the " forward " franc discount had passed the 35 per cent mark in terms of annual interest rates. From June 1 to June 22, moreover, the Exchange Stabilization Fund lost about 5.2 billion francs in a vain attempt to bolster the exchange rate of the franc, and between June 22 and June 28 it spent another 2.5 billions; of the total of 7.7 billions, about 4 billions had to be loaned to the Fund by the Bank of France.

The committee in charge of the Fund recommended drastic fiscal reforms to ease the exchange situation, but its suggestions were rejected by the government on June 14; MM. Rist and Baudouin, two of the four members, resigned in protest, whereupon the agitation in the Paris money-market increased. Ten days later Blum asked the legislature for decree-making powers to deal with the panic; rebuffed by the Senate, he and his government resigned.

PROSPERITY UNREGAINED

Wholesale and retail price movements.—The most striking change in business conditions during the first four months of the Popular Front régime was a drastic increase in wholesale and retail prices. After falling almost without interruption since the spring of 1929, wholesale prices in France had reached a low in the summer of 1935. From then until Feb-

CHART 7. Prices and Exchange Rates, 1929-1939

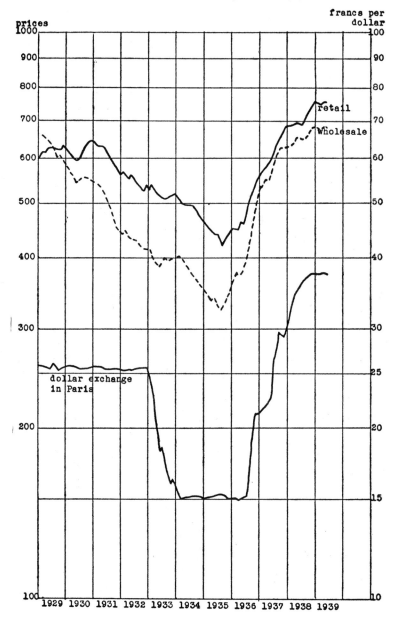

SOURCE: *SGF*. For retail prices, July, 1914 = 100; for wholesale
prices, 1913 = 100.

ruary, 1936, the general wholesale price index rose from 322 to 372; from February to June, 1936, prices were steady.[39] But one month after the Popular Front government was formed an inflationary spiral was unleashed which matched in intensity those of 1919-1920 and 1926.

The wholesale price index climbed from 378 in June to 471 in October, 1936, a rise of about 25 per cent. A steep rate of increase was continued through the second phase of the Popular Front; the general index of wholesale prices reached 550 in March, 1937. Increases in wholesale prices registered *after* October, 1936 were partly attributable to the devaluation. But price increases *before* the devaluation, which appeared in spite of a business slump, demonstrated that the " reflationary " efforts of the Popular Front were taken up in higher prices rather than in a general business revival.

The policy of raising agricultural prices by government action, begun during the depression by the " deflationary " governments, was continued by the Popular Front in spite of the general price rise in the second half of 1936. The " Interprofessional Council of the National Wheat Office," created by the law of August 15, 1936 to fix the monthly purchase price of wheat, allowed a 60 per cent increase between October, 1936 and May, 1937. Wine and hay prices rose by about the same amount; meat, sugar, and dairy products rose about 30 per cent over the same period.[40] In other countries the price rise in foodstuffs in 1936 was only one-fifth to one-third that in France.[41]

The contemporary outcry against " fraudulent " price boosts in retail shops [42] is a sign that many shopkeepers were not

39 SGF, index of 126 articles, 1913 = 100.

40 *La France économique en 1936*, pp. 511-512.

41 *L'Activité économique*, 1936, p. 282.

42 Which eventually resulted in some rather ineffectual attempts at price fixing.

waiting to be forced to raise their prices by higher replacement costs. Deflation and falling prices were associated in everybody's mind with the conservative governments of 1934 and 1935; the country expected higher prices to prevail now that an "anti-deflationist" government was in power. The memory of the distress caused by the price inflation in 1925 and 1926 was too fresh for many to resist following the lead of the first nervous merchants who marked up their prices.

The result was that retail prices swung up almost as sharply and as rapidly as did wholesale prices. The index of the cost of living, reflecting the rise in retail prices, jumped from 80.3 just before the Blum government took office to 99.4 one year later, virtually equalling the high cost of living of the prosperity years 1930-1931.[43] A further rise in the cost of living was restrained by the politically expedient move of allowing the decree-law of July 16, 1935, which had lowered rents by 10 per cent, to remain in force.[44]

Income and employment under the Popular Front.—The failure of Popular Front economic and financial experiments is brought out most clearly by an examination of changes in national income in 1936 and 1937. According to the estimates of Dugé de Bernonville, French national income rose from 175 billion francs in 1935 to 201 billions in 1936 and to 242 billions in 1937 (38 per cent increase over the whole period). At the same time the cost of living in France rose about 37 per cent. Another estimate [45] of national income, in terms of constant (1938) prices, is as follows:

> *1929—391 billion francs*
> 1935—324 billion francs
> 1936—320 billion francs
> 1937—331 billion francs

43 *SGF*, 1930 = 100.

44 *La France économique en 1936*, p. 517.

45 Froment and Gavanier.

For the nation as a whole, therefore, increases in income tended to be wiped out by the steep rises in prices. On the other hand, Dr. M. Kalecki has demonstrated that *shifts* in purchasing power did occur as a result of the Popular Front experiment.[46]

Kalecki estimates that between April, 1936 and April, 1937 there was an increase of 57 per cent in payments to labor for wage increases, paid holidays, and a shorter work week.[47] Since at the same time there was a 27 per cent increase in the cost of living, Kalecki finds that French labor *as a whole* gained 24 per cent in real income.[48] But some of this gain was due to a drop in partial unemployment; individual laborers, working a fewer number of hours, gained on the average only 28 per cent in terms of monetary units, therefore earning only 1 per cent more in real income.

For salaried and professional employees Kalecki finds an increase in money wages of about 24 per cent on the average, making for a slight fall in real income to April, 1937. Those on fixed incomes suffered the worst decline in real income (17 per cent), offset only slightly by the annulment of some of Laval's deflationary measures by the Blum government. In agriculture and small business, changes in income were almost exactly paralleled by increases in the cost of living. The lion's share of the increase in national money income, therefore, went to the owners of large scale commercial and industrial enterprises, members of precisely that class which was most hostile to the Blum régime.

46 " The Lessons of the Blum Experiment," *Economic Journal*, March, 1938, pp. 31-36.

47 A French source enumerates the increases in payments to labor for the period June, 1936-June, 1937 as follows: 21-25 per cent for the " Matignon Accords " which helped settle the first wave of " sit-down " strikes, 4-6 per cent for paid vacations, 12 per cent for arbitration awards to labor (after December, 1936), and 20 per cent for the forty-hour week, or a total of about 60 per cent. (*La France économique en 1936*, pp. 278-279.)

48 $157/127 = 124$.

The dearth of scholarly French monographs dealing with the effects of the Blum experiments on the French economy is surprising and discouraging. We do possess one interesting study on wages and working conditions in Alsace during this period.[49] According to this study, the established average hourly minimum wage in a large Strasbourg textile factory rose as follows :[50]

July, 1929	*4.69 francs*
November, 1936	4.99
January, 1937	5.98
July, 1937	6.47

During the Blum régime, therefore, the minimum hourly wage in this factory rose about 38 per cent. Over the same period, the index of the cost of living in the *département* which includes Strasbourg (Bas-Rhin) rose about 27 per cent.[51] Braun's observations of the standard of living in Alsace indicate that there was little change in the real income of the average worker there.[52] The working class in this area did benefit as a whole from the forty-hour law; unemployed workers on public relief rolls in the *département* of Bas-Rhin fell from 4,200 in January, 1936 to 600 in December, 1937.[53]

The forty-hour week, generally in force in all French establishments of over one hundred employees by May, 1937, lowered the average work week about 13 per cent. According to one estimate, it would have been impossible to compensate for this loss in national working time by hiring workers previously unemployed. There were in 1937 about 675,000 idle

49 André Braun, *L'Ouvrier alsacien et l'expérience du front populaire* (Paris: Recueil Sirey, 1938).

50 *Ibid.*, pp. 18-21.

51 *SGF*, 1930 = 100.

52 Braun, *op. cit.*, p. 50. There was, of course, an increase in leisure time; many Alsatian workers used this to supplement their incomes with "black labor" (*travail noir*), that is, by filling two or more jobs.

53 *Ibid.*, p. 51.

workers of all categories in France, of whom 300,000 were considered unemployable. Even if all the remaining 375,000 unemployed had been absorbed, this would have raised total hours worked only 5.5 per cent, since the total labor force involved was on the order of 6,775,000 workers. Providing full-time work for all who were only partially employed might have meant an additional increase of 2.5 per cent in man-hours. This still would have meant replacement of only 8/13 or 62 per cent of total working hours cut off by the forty-hour law.[54]

Actually, French industry did not engage in any large-scale hiring to compensate for time lost because of the forty-hour week. Foreign workers were not used to any great extent to make up the deficiency. Only 16,281 additional immigrant workers were admitted in 1936 and 70,672 in 1937, while in 1930 the comparable number had been 177,830.[55] A constant complaint voiced by French employers was the lack of available skilled labor after the beginning of 1937.[56] Coal mining, iron and steel, aluminum goods, machine tools, and motor manufacture were among those industries which claimed to be unable to fill orders because of the dearth of skilled workmen.[57] There are conflicting reports on whether the efficiency of French labor per man-hour declined with the appearance of the Popular Front.[58] But it cannot be denied that application of the forty-hour law between November, 1936 and May, 1937 coincided with the downturn in industrial production after the slight revival accompanying the 1936 devaluation.

54 *L'Activité économique*, 1938, pp. 24-25.

55 *L'Evolution de l'économie française*, Table 7.

56 Commission of Inquiry into Production, *JO, Annex*, December 18, 1937.

57 Robert Marjolin, " Reflections on the Blum Experiment," *Economica*, May, 1938, pp. 185-186.

58 According to a report of the *Comité des houilles*, there was a drop of 6.6 per cent in the average hourly output of miners. See *L'Activité économique*, 1936, p. 275. But Kalecki (*op. cit.*, p. 27) and Braun (*op. cit.*, pp. 25-26) found no decrease in labor productivity at this time.

Exchange rates under the Popular Front.—With the monetary law of October 1 the gold bullion standard was reluctantly abandoned. To the French this monetary standard had had cherished associations with the Poincaré *assainissement* and the prosperous years of 1928 to 1930. It would have been politically inexpedient to have admitted to the *rentiers* that this was the definitive end of the gold standard. " At some time in the future," according to the law, another gold value for the franc would be set. Meanwhile the " elastic " franc would be restricted in the scope of its movements; but within 43 and 49 milligrams of gold per franc there could be the " free interplay of economic and financial forces on the money-market."

The gold limits of the " elastic " franc, however, implied no obligation on the part of the central bank to redeem its banknotes at any rate whatsoever. They were limits only in the sense that the Exchange Stabilization Fund was committed to limiting within them fluctuations in the *equivalent* exchange value of the franc with other currencies which were still on gold. The Tripartite Monetary Pact, moreover, was small comfort to those Frenchmen who regarded a definite amount of yellow metal as the necessary basis for any sound currency system. According to the terms of this pact, the signatories were not obliged to give each other more than twenty-four hours notice before changing their selling or buying price for gold.[59]

With the devaluation of September, 1936, fluctuations of the forward franc became a matter of increasing importance in the making of French monetary policy. Previously forward exchange had been a means of preventing losses in international currency transactions and only incidentally a field of operations for a small group of highly-specialized cambists. Now that the protection of a specific gold parity for the " spot " franc was re-

[59] According to an agreement signed October 13, 1936. The Tripartite agreement allowed the exchange stabilization funds of all signatories to draw on the gold reserves of other funds and central banks. The British Exchange Equalisation Account, for example, was allowed to purchase French gold even though France was off the gold standard.

moved, the forward exchange market became a battlefield for speculators and the controllers of the Exchange Stabilization Fund.

The franc had been quoted at a discount against the pound sterling at three months ever since the beginning of 1935. By June, 1936, the national elections, the "sit-down" strikes, and the frightening international events had driven the forward franc down to a discount of more than 7.00 francs per pound.[60] The government's repeated pronouncements in favor of maintaining the Poincaré franc lowered the discount to about 2.38 francs per pound, but in September rumors of devaluation raised it again to 8.34 francs per pound.

The September devaluation reduced the "spot" rate of the franc from 6.6 to 4.7 cents, and the Exchange Stabilization Fund managed to keep it at this rate for four months. The initial reflux of émigré capital which followed the devaluation wiped out the discount on the forward franc, but in the following months a substantial discount appeared once more; after January, 1937, the Fund had to shovel all of its reserves into the breach in a vain attempt to fight off the speculative attack against the franc which developed from the new wave of distrust in the Popular Front administration.

In the third phase of the Blum régime the committee of experts in charge of the Fund bought temporary relief from speculative attacks by allowing the franc to sink to the equivalent of its lower limit, 43 milligrams of gold. The franc promptly dropped to 4.4 cents, and the forward discounts slackened off. But the financial panic in June, 1937, which ended the short career of the Auriol franc, saw the appearance of an enormous discount of 9.50 francs per pound.

The Popular Front and the money-market.—The years previous to the Popular Front had had their monetary crises, but none when the *rentiers* felt so unjustly hounded by the op-

---

60 Bank of France, *Cours des changes*. Since the exchange rate of the pound sterling was 76.16 francs in June, this represented a discount of about 37 per cent in terms of annual interest rates. See Chart 6.

pressor-State as in 1936. In spite of repeated promises on the part of the government, the exchange value of their hoards of bonds and bank-notes had been cut, and their savings were dwindling in value each month because of the inflationary measures enacted by the Popular Front. To add to their difficulties, the *rentiers* were forbidden to ship gold abroad or even to benefit from the increased monetary value of gold.

Given the individualism and anti-étatist bias of the French, it was inevitable that this irritating situation would result in strenuous attempts to be quit of all holdings expressed in monetary units. A drastic decline in the value of government securities outstanding demonstrated the *rentiers'* lack of confidence in the future of the franc. In June, 1936 the value of Treasury bonds outstanding (including those held by the Bank as well as those held by private banks and individuals) amounted to 18.5 billion francs. By the time of the October devaluation they had dropped to only 6.8 billions, and they reached a low of 4.8 billions just before the Blum government was forced to resign (June, 1937).[61]

With less money available from banks and private investors, the government was forced to turn to the central bank. Bank of France advances to the government again became an issue in French political life, as in the years after the First World War. The 1928 devaluation and the successful financial management of the Poincaré administration had wiped out the government's debt to the Bank, to the great satisfaction of all concerned. Only a small "permanent loan" to the State had remained. Now, in order to carry out a large program of public works and to rebuild the country's war machine, the Popular Front governments and their successors were forced to renew the practice of borrowing directly from the Bank of France.

In his speech to the Chamber of Deputies on June 19, 1936, Vincent Auriol revealed that previous governments, beginning with the Laval régime in 1935, had borrowed money from the

61 Vigreux, *op. cit.*, p. 132.

Bank via a " detour." Laval had persuaded the Bank to accept short-term Treasury bonds for discount. Some 13.8 billions of francs had been loaned in this manner by the Bank.[62] Auriol declared that the Popular Front government, " publicly, directly, without shame, without hypocrisy," would ask instead for direct loans from the Bank.[63] A convention was arranged between Bank and State (June 18, 1936) [64] whereby the Treasury bonds discounted by the Bank would be redeemed as they fell due, and the total sum of 13.8 billions made available to the State in the form of interest-free loans. The old controversy over whether the Bank of France should or should not be *required* to discount *bons* was settled by the law of July 24, 1936 obligating the Bank to discount all short-term liabilities of the Treasury which were within three months of maturity.[65]

The column " avances provisoires à l'Etat " thereupon reappeared in the weekly Bank of France report, after an absence of nine years. In June, 1936 the State borrowed 536 million francs from the Bank. The amount of advances increased by 5.7 billion francs in July, to 9.2 billions in August, and to 15.9 billions in September. The monetary law of October 1 reduced Bank-to-State advances by using seven billion francs of the unearned increase in the value of the Bank's metallic reserves. But by the end of October Bank-to-State advances had increased again to 12.3 billions; in December the total was up to 17.7 billions and in January, 1937 to 20.0 billions, where it remained until the overthrow of the Blum government.

While the government was borrowing heavily for its increased needs, private investment was fading away. The bank-

62 In reply to Auriol's speech, Laval's associates declared that this arrangement had not been secret and that in fact the transactions had been regularly reported to the legislative finance committees; nevertheless, it is true that most of the French were unaware that their government had been getting these disguised advances from the Bank.

63 *JO, Débats, Chambre,* 1936, pp. 1500-1509.

64 *JO, Lois et Décrets,* 1936, p. 6586.

65 Laufenburger, *op. cit.,* pp. 304-305.

ing community showed itself very reluctant to extend credit in view of the unsettled political conditions.[66] New issues of French stocks and bonds fell off in 1936 to less than half of their average monthly value in the depression year 1935, and it was not until after the period of the " pause " that investment in French industry began to show definite signs of improvement.[67] During 1936 and 1937 the government borrowed virtually all national savings which did not flee the country or go into hoards.

For the ordinary citizen, the only avenue of escape from the forces threatening his savings was " amateur speculation " in hoarded gold, real estate, and other commodities. The speculator, of course, could express his distrust in the future of the franc more directly through purchases of foreign currencies in the still-free foreign exchange market.

As in 1935, the deflationary effect of the capital flight was counterbalanced by the new advances of currency from the Bank of France. But the volume of note circulation was remarkably restrained in view of the immense sums borrowed by the government from the Bank of France. The twenty billions of " extraordinary " advances cannot all be considered *additional* advances from the Bank, since almost fourteen billions merely replaced the amount in *bons* which had been discounted by the Bank of France for the preceding governments. This leaves six billion francs as additional advances to the Blum government; but even these advances did not show up as increases in the Bank of France note circulation. All through the Blum régime the total volume of bank-notes in circulation fluctuated only slightly about a level of eighty-six billion francs. The lack of any substantial increase in the volume of currency is all the more noteworthy in view of the rise in price levels which must have caused a larger monetary stock to be required by the busi-

66 League of Nations, *Aperçu de la situation monétaire* (Geneva, 1936), p. 148.

67 NBER, 10,33.

ness community. The obvious explanation is that the Exchange Stabilization Fund was forced to accept such large quantities of francs from bearish speculators that the total volume of note circulation remained fairly stable. There is, of course, little direct information to be had on the secret operations of the Fund, but we do know that it had to spend ten billion francs in gold in 1936 and another seven billions in the first half of 1937.

In the years 1936-1937, in other words, the francs advanced by the Bank to the State were the same as had been turned over to the Bank by the Fund, which in turn had had to absorb these francs from French speculators. In the monetary crises of 1925 and 1926, on the other hand, increases in Bank advances had resulted in proportionate increases in note circulation because the Bank had refused then to sell gold; the inflationary effect of the advances had not been counterbalanced by gold exports. The relationship of note circulation and advances in the two periods is quite different.

NOTE CIRCULATION AND BANK OF FRANCE ADVANCES
Coefficients of Correlation (Monthly observations)

Poincaré stabilization:
    September, 1925–December, 1926 .... + .93
    January, 1927–April, 1928 .... — .63
Popular Front devaluations:
    June, 1936–July, 1937 .... + .58
    August, 1937–November, 1938 .... + .28

In spite of the success of a guaranteed bond issue in March, 1937, low tax receipts and increased public expenditures created a situation during the Popular Front's third phase in which the French Treasury had just enough funds to meet its payments, provided that the value of short-term *bons du Trésor* and *bons de la Défense nationale* outstanding did not fall off. For the last eight months of 1937 the Treasury had about 20.3 billion francs of foreseeable expenses to meet, with only 6.3 billions on hand and legislative authority to raise 15 billions in *bons du Trésor* and 2.5 billions in *bons de la Dé-*

fense nationale.[68] For the continued existence of the Blum régime, "confidence," represented by the willingness of the money-market to absorb enough new short-term government bonds to replace those falling due, was of the essence. When this mark of confidence was withheld, Blum had to ask for financial decree-making powers; when they were denied him, he had no alternative but to resign.

SOME OBSERVATIONS ON THE BLUM EXPERIMENTS

The character of the crisis which overthrew the Blum government in June, 1937 is itself a commentary on the remarkable extent to which Popular Front monetary and financial policy had changed by that time. The panic of June, 1937 was completely within the financial sphere and had no direct connection with the basic social and economic aims of the Popular Front. Trouble generated in the forward exchange market moved over to the political arena when Blum asked for decree-making powers to deal with the panic. The Senate, which overthrew the Blum government by refusing to grant these powers, would probably have agreed to the same demand twelve months previously.

The experiments in increasing purchasing power launched in June, 1936 were founded on the belief that a general business revival would inevitably entrain financial and fiscal improvement. By September this position had been modified so that a "monetary manipulation"—devaluation—replaced "reflation" as the mechanism for stimulating economic expansion. During the period of the "pause," all further social, economic, and financial reforms were abandoned for the express purpose of appeasing the forces which were damaging the exchange position of the franc.

The failure of the French economy to show any definite signs of improvement was responsible for forcing the Blum government to change its monetary policies so drastically. One year after coming to power the Popular Front leaders had been

68 *L'Activité économique,* 1937, p. 108.

maneuvered into a position where a stable exchange rate was
the criterion of their success; that accomplished, the rapid defeat of the government was a certainty, since the men who made
up the exchange market—those who bought and sold in the
Bourse and at the foreign exchange departments of the banks
—were the very men who had the most to fear from Blum's
policies. The Popular Front placed its future in the hands of
its enemies.

The problem of why the Blum government refused to institute exchange control against speculation is complex. Devaluation, which was expressly in opposition to the Popular
Front program, was finally adopted; on the other hand, the
Communists and left-wing Socialists, supports of the Popular
Front, argued in vain for the adoption of exchange control.
At least one economist believes refusal to introduce exchange
control was one of the chief causes of the Popular Front's
failure.[69] It is possible that Blum rejected exchange control
because he feared the United States and Great Britain would
resent such a unilateral action, or perhaps because, having once
so vehemently rejected devaluation, he was reluctant to do
another about-face on the subject of exchange control.

The monetary and economic policies of this Blum government contained a fatal contradiction. It proved impossible to
effect basic reforms at one stroke within the framework of
existing liberal capitalistic institutions. Given a free foreign
exchange market, for example, it was impossible to persuade
financiers to keep their funds in the French economy and to
enforce the forty-hour week at the same time. The appeasement of the entrepreneurs during the last months of the Blum
government was an admission that in a capitalist system it is
the actions and reactions of the industrialists, merchants,
bankers, and speculators that affect the swings of the business

69 Kalecki, *op. cit.*, p. 39. But there is reason to believe that if Blum had
instituted exchange control at this time, France would have been subjected
to a debilitating black market in *devisen* similar to that which she experienced between 1941 and 1949.

cycle most vitally; the State can do relatively little to effect an economic revival in opposition to the will of the entrepreneurial class.

Just as the French speculator refused to be cajoled into an acceptance of the exchange value of the Auriol franc, the French industrialist refused to expand his output except on his own terms. Even before the inauguration of the forty-hour week, French manufacturers did not respond to the stimulus of rising prices by increasing their production. It is quite possible that the forty-hour law did help to aggravate industrial stagnation by reducing the expansive capacity of the French economy. But it is doubtful that the manufacturer who refused to increase production in the face of rising prices during the first half of the Blum régime would have acted much differently if the forty-hour week law had never been enacted.

The French Left, disgruntled by the failure of the Popular Front to produce a satisfactory business revival, accused the business leaders of sabotaging the Popular Front with a " sit-down strike of capital " and of being the victims of a " collective psychosis." [70] But whether or not the entrepreneurs were impelled by political rather than economic motives, the effects of their decisions were of direct importance for the French economy.

70 *La France économique en 1936*, p. 776.

CHAPTER VI
THE RETURN TO CONFIDENCE

The Paper Franc, 1937-1939

" There is not a single Frenchman who has funds he cannot immediately use," said Charles Rist, commenting in 1938 on the financial aftermath of the Blum experiments, " who does not reflect whether it might be safer to send them abroad than to keep them home." The Paris money-market had been so demoralized that it could be expected to play its necessary role only upon the appearance of "a more intelligent financial policy," *i.e.*, a return to the principles of financial and economic orthodoxy.[1] Demands for the abandonment of the Popular Front monetary and economic policies became more insistent after the fall of the Blum administration in June, 1937 had signalized the failure of its attempts to achieve prosperity.

Gradually the succeeding governments became more and more conservative. Once the government had accepted a stable franc as the criterion of its success, it was logical that it should try to change the direction of economic and monetary policy to suit the opinions of French banking and financial interests.

The internal history of France from 1937 to the outbreak of the war, therefore, was primarily involved with a shift away from the original social and economic policies of the Popular Front. Politically, this was manifested in the shift of the balance of executive and legislative power from the extreme Left to a coalition of Center and Right. Socially, it involved an increasingly hostile attitude toward the activities of labor unions, culminating in modification of the forty-hour week. In the financial realm, the partisans of financial orthodoxy and " confidence " gradually gained the day. This new direction of French monetary policy, evident to some degree in the first Chautemps government of 1937, was clearly in the ascendancy

1 " The Financial Situation of France," *Foreign Affairs,* July, 1938, p. 606.

during the second Chautemps administration (January—April, 1938) and the first Daladier administration (May—November, 1938). During the Daladier-Reynaud administration from November, 1938 to the outbreak of war, return to more conservative fiscal and monetary policies finally succeeded in bringing back a certain measure of financial stability.

The Popular Front " à direction radicale."—The Blum experiment came to an end with the formation of the second Popular Front government on June 24, 1937. The Radical-Socialist and Socialist parties collaborated, as before, in the ministry; once again the Communists lent their more or less grudging support. But the relationship of the two chief parties was reversed. This time the Radicals took the key ministerial posts. Chautemps, noted for his facility at working with dissident parliamentary factions, became the head of the new government. Léon Blum was relegated to the post of vice premier, and Georges Bonnet replaced Vincent Auriol as minister of finance.

The new government was faced by the same financial panic that had precipitated the overthrow of its predecessor. On the basis of the obvious necessity for quick and drastic action, Chautemps asked for and received the decree-making powers which had been refused Blum. Awarded until August 31, 1937, Chautemps' *pleins-pouvoirs* had as their objectives: ". . . the suppression of attacks on State credit, the fight against speculation, economic recovery, price control, budgetary equilibrium and stability of the Treasury, and defense of the reserves of the Bank of France without exchange control.[2]

The shift away from the earlier social and economic objectives of the Popular Front was not abrupt. In July, 1937, for example, Georges Bonnet found it necessary to defend the government's financial policies on the ground that financial stability was necessary *in order to defend* the advances made during the first year of the Popular Front.[3]

2 *JO, Lois et Décrets*, 1937, p. 7418.

3 *Le Temps*, July 1, 1937.

Agitated discussion on the effects of the forty-hour week led to the formation of a government Committee of Inquiry on Production in August, 1937. The report of this committee (December 16, 1937) settled nothing. It proved a much more cautious analysis of the situation than had been expected by opponents of the forty-hour week. The committee found that in spite of employers' complaints, the social laws of the Blum government had resulted in no appreciable reduction of the productivity per man-hour of individual laborers. Its report recommended that exceptions to the forty-hour week law should be made in the national defense industries, coal and iron mines, and seasonal industries, but only with very definite accompanying safeguards to labor for the proper payment of overtime work.[4] The government should help relieve the shortage of skilled labor, the report suggested, by improving the existing employment service and by providing funds for training apprentices; the lag in French production could be offset somewhat by interest-free, government-sponsored loans for plant modernization and re-equipment.

The " Bonnet franc."—During June the franc had been the victim of a powerful speculative attack based on the obvious inability of the French Exchange Stabilization Fund to maintain it at the 43-milligram minimum gold rate which had been set by the law of October 1, 1936. The discount on the three-month forward rate of the franc against sterling had jumped from 1.74 francs per pound in May, 1937 to 9.50 francs in June, at the height of the crisis.[5] The comparable forward discount per dollar had risen from .40 to 1.97 francs. In terms of annual interest rates, this meant an advantage of over 37 per cent to holders of forward sterling or dollars.[6] At the end of June, the minister of finance revealed that during that one month the Stabilization Fund had lost about 7.7 billions in

4 *Ibid.*, December 20, 1937.

5 Bank of France, *Cours des changes.* See Chart 6.

6 Vigreux, *op. cit.*, p. 58.

gold (of which 4.0 billions had been borrowed from the Bank of France) in attempting to offset this speculative pressure.[7] The harassed government decided to abandon the gold minimum for the franc established in October, 1936. Operations in the money-market were suspended on June 29, and the next day, by virtue of a decree-law, a new devaluation was accomplished. The Auriol franc had had a career of nine months.

The new " Bonnet franc " was also known as the " floating franc." It was not attached to a specific amount of gold (as was the Poincaré franc) ; nor was it limited to a set minimum and maximum (as was the " elastic " Auriol franc). The government simply announced that " at some future date " a new gold exchange value would be set for the franc.[8] Meanwhile the Exchange Stabilization Fund was retained and its powers and privileges reaffirmed. But henceforth, as Bonnet announced, it would be committed only to a " mobile defense of the franc." For all practical purposes the franc was now " simply an abstract unit of account, detached from all material elements, notably gold." [9]

In order to anticipate and offset international repercussions of this devaluation, the French government made use of the "Tripartite " apparatus set up just before the 1936 devaluation. The American and British governments officially recognized that, in view of the speculative pressure on the franc, devaluation had been forced upon France and was not undertaken with a view toward achieving " an advantage of exchange " of an undervalued position, which would tend to create a favorable balance of payments.[10]

Following the classic pattern for devaluation, the reserves of precious metal at the central bank were revalued in terms

7 Pirou, *Traité*, p. 329.

8 *JO, Débats, Chambre*, 1937, pp. 2069-2072.

9 F. Moliexe, *Le Système monétaire français (son évolution depuis 1936)* (Paris: Jouve et Cie., 1942), p. 56.

10 *Le Temps*, July 5, 1937.

of new francs, and the unearned increment placed at the disposition of the State. The devaluation of October, 1936 had revalued the Bank's gold reserves at the rate of 49 milligrams per franc; the devaluation of June 30, 1937 revalued them at 43 milligrams, so that in effect what had been the minimum gold limit of the " elastic franc " became the maximum for the " floating franc." [11] The resulting additional resources of seven billion francs were turned over to the newly-created " Bond Defense Fund " (*Fonds de soutien des rentes*). This institution was to function as an adjunct of the Treasury, purchasing government long and medium-term issues when their prices dropped too low, in order to create confidence in the financial market.[12]

The Chautemps decree-laws.—In two other series of decree-laws (July 20 and 31) Chautemps attempted to ease the desperate position of the French Treasury, which found its assets reduced to a total of only 20 million francs as of June 29, 1937. The business turnover tax was supplemented by a new " tax on production," the general income tax rates were raised, and railroad fares were increased. Protective tariffs, which had been lowered about 15 per cent during the Blum administration, were now raised to their previous level in an effort to cut France's unfavorable balance of trade and to provide the Treasury with additional revenue. Also included, possibly for their supposed moral value, were the standard gestures toward " suppression of fiscal fraud " and a rather improbable 100 per cent tax on speculative profits made during the recent

11 Convention of July 21, 1937 between the Bank of France, and the government.

12 *JO, Lois et Décrets*, 1937, pp. 8334-8335. For an explanation of the functioning of this institution see *Le Temps*, July 26, 1937. Even after the addition of the Bond Defense Fund to her financial institutions, France still did not engage in " open-market " transactions as they were understood in England and the United States. Only on June 17, 1938, when the Bank of France was allowed to buy and sell *short-term* bonds and commercial paper on the open market, did the Bank have open-market powers similar to those of the Bank of England and the Federal Reserve System. (*JO, Lois et Décrets*, 1938, p. 7443.)

financial panic. The " ordinary budget " for 1937, which had been left unbalanced by the Blum government because of its " transitional " nature, was now put into balance, at least on paper. The conservative opponents of the Popular Front were quick to point out, however, that all this budget-balancing was accomplished by increasing governmental revenue rather than by effecting any considerable budgetary trimming.

In August, 1937, just before the expiration of its decree-making powers, the Chautemps government nationalized the remaining major private railroad systems. A decree-law to this effect was issued partly in the hope that with a more rationalized railway network France would be spared some of its burdensome yearly railway deficit. The State now accepted financial responsibility for its railroads until 1943, when, it was assumed, the French railroad system would be self-supporting.

The fate of the " floating franc."—The devaluation of June 30, 1937 and the " *trains* " of decree-laws which followed had little lasting effect on " confidence." In the opinion of the French entrepreneurial class, the disturbing factors introduced by the first Popular Front government had not been mitigated sufficiently.[13] Specifically, the load of the French budget remained too heavy, and the forty-hour work week was still in effect. On June 25, 1937, one day after coming to power, the Chautemps government was threatened with a serious strike which was avoided only when the forty-hour week was extended to hotel and restaurant workers. In September, 1937, after much heart-searching, the Radical-Socialist party voted to continue its support for the social and economic reforms of the Popular Front.[14] Other unsettling factors were the fear of a world war resulting from the Spanish Civil War and the continued absence of a real business revival, in spite of the precipitous climb of prices. Furthermore, the desperate posi-

13 See the lead editorials in *Le Temps* for August 24 and September 12, 1937; also *Le Temps financier* for August 16 and September 6, 1937.

14 *Le Temps*, September 11, 1937.

tion of the Treasury became apparent to all when the "extraordinary" advances of the Bank of France were increased by about five billion francs in October and by an equal amount in December.

The continuation of an atmosphere of social tension, financial mistrust, and political uncertainty meant the continuation of an irresistible speculative pressure against the franc. After dropping from 110 to 129 per pound and from 22.46 to 26.26 per dollar at the time of the 1937 devaluation, the franc became the victim of another sustained "bear" attack in September, 1937. Once again the forward discount on the franc passed the 30 per cent mark in terms of interest rates. In October appeared the highest forward premium in francs on sterling ever recorded before the Second World War: 11.50 francs per pound.[15]

Rather than have this "attack" result in another depletion of France's gold reserves, the Exchange Stabilization Fund allowed the exchange rate to slip downward in the hope that adverse speculation would cease when the franc adjusted itself "to its true situation."[16] In September the franc fell to 147 per pound sterling and to 28.36 per dollar. Since the end of the first Popular Front government it had depreciated by about 26 per cent. It was worth, in terms of gold equivalents, only about 45 per cent of the Poincaré franc and 10 per cent of the pre-war *Germinal* franc.

At the beginning of October, 1937, when the seasonal decline of the tourist industry made the exchange position of the franc extremely critical, the Council of Ministers was called to the President's summer chateau at Rambouillet, whence came an urgent official announcement designed to have a "psychological shock" on "confidence." The burden of the "Declaration of Rambouillet" was that there was no objective or "technical" reason for the speculative attack on the franc. The Council of Ministers emphasized its determination to deal

15 Bank of France, *Cours des changes.*

16 *Le Temps,* October 1, 1937.

firmly with the current outbreak of strikes and to settle the country's economic and financial problems without recourse to exchange control. It called upon France to end the attack on the franc " by the unanimous national will to defend its prosperity through work, discipline, and union." [17] This definition of government policy, with its implied assurances against a return to the aggressive days of the Popular Front, produced an immediate and favorable reaction in the Paris money-market.[18]

Additional support for the exchange position of the franc came from an unexpected source: the stock market crash in New York a few weeks after the " Declaration of Rambouillet." The crash, and the world-wide business recession which accompanied it, started a flow of " hot money " to France. This inflow of capital was the first of any size since the establishment of the Auriol franc. In November and December the Exchange Stabilization Fund had no difficulty in maintaining the franc at a level of about 145 per pound sterling, and the premium on forward sterling fell to about 2.00-2.50 francs per pound. The demand for francs was such that on November 18, to the accompaniment of a great deal of publicity, the Fund was able to turn 3.1 billion francs in gold over to the Bank of France.[19] But the end of 1937 saw the end of these favorable factors behind the movement of capital, which had never been able to reach very considerable proportions.

The end of the Popular Front.—By the beginning of 1938, political and economic conditions in France were once more in a state of crisis. The world depression at this time caused a drop in French exports and in industrial production, even while French prices, under the influence of the depreciating exchange, continued to rise. The government proved powerless to deal

17 *Ibid.*, October 3, 1937.

18 Vigreux, *op. cit.*, p. 61.

19 Due to the depreciation of the franc since the June 30, 1937 devaluation, the amount of gold handed over to the Bank was really worth about four billion current francs.

with another wave of strikes which broke out in the last weeks of 1937, even though Chautemps threatened to use force to oust "sit-down" strikers.[20] On January 13 Chautemps and the Communist wing of the Popular Front clashed bitterly over his attitude toward the strikes; because of this challenge to the labor movement the Socialist ministers felt obliged to withdraw from the government, and Chautemps resigned. After a fruitless attempt on the part of Georges Bonnet to form a new government with himself as head, the premiership was offered again to Chautemps, who succeeded in forming the third Popular Front government—this time minus several key Socialist leaders, including Blum.

This new government proved completely incapable of controlling the rapidly deteriorating monetary situation. At the end of January, 1938 the pound jumped from 150 to 155 francs, and the three months forward discount on francs again reached 11.00 francs for sterling and 2.25 francs for dollars. During February the position of the Treasury once again became desperate, and the advances of the Bank of France to the State were increased by 6.5 billion francs, to a grand total of 38.5 billions. In March Chautemps went before the legislature to ask for another grant of decree-making powers, and a political crisis resulted when the Socialists refused to lend their support to this project. This was the moment chosen by Hitler for the *Anschluss* with Austria.

On March 13, 1938 Léon Blum formed the fourth and last Popular Front government; on that day the pound sterling jumped from 156 to 162 francs.[21] Blum tried to avoid controversial financial and labor issues and appealed for unity in the face of the menacing international situation. But he also was finally forced to ask for financial decree-making powers; refusal by the Senate once more precipitated a government crisis.

20 *Le Temps,* December 25, 1932.

21 *Ibid.,* March 14, 1938.

One month after the formation of Blum's second administration, a new ministry was organized by Edouard Daladier, this time from a coalition of Radical-Socialists and most of the groupings on the Right. The Popular Front was effectively ended by this split between the Socialists and the Radicals.[22] For the remaining months of peace this same coalition of Center and Right ruled France. " The pernicious ideologies are now abandoned," observed the lead editorial of *Le Temps* for April 27, 1938.

The " sterling franc."—The Daladier régime, immediately provided with decree-making powers, proceeded to the fourth and last inter-war devaluation of the franc. On May 4, 1938 Daladier announced that the long-continued depreciation of the franc would be brought to a halt. Henceforth, he said, the minimum exchange rate of the franc would be fixed at about 179 per pound sterling, " a base which can be defended victoriously." [23] In effect, this was a further devaluation of about 38 per cent, since the pound had been selling for about 130 francs just before the devaluation of June 30, 1937. From the end of World War I to the beginning of World War II the French franc had lost more than nine-tenths of its original gold equivalent.

TABLE 6

VALUE OF THE FRANC IN MILLIGRAMS OF GOLD

(900/1000 fine)

1914	" *Germinal* "	322.58
June, 1928	" Poincaré "	65.5
October, 1936	" Auriol; elastic "	49.0
July, 1937	" Bonnet; floating "	43.0
May, 1938	" sterling "	27.6

22 Although it was not until their party congress in November, 1938 that the Radical-Socialists formally decided to withdraw from the " Rassemblement populaire."

23 See the text of Daladier's radio speech in *Le Temps*, May 6, 1938.

Another devaluation, another name: after May, 1938 the " Bonnet " or " floating franc " became the " sterling franc," since its standard was a more or less fixed amount of sterling exchange.[24] The " repli " (turning) demanded by Daladier became a fact; the franc was maintained at the rate of 179 francs or less per pound from May, 1938 until the outbreak of war. At the same time, however, the pound sterling itself was becoming depreciated in terms of gold or dollars, in the face of war scares in 1938 and 1939; the franc declined from 2.81 American cents in May, 1938 to 2.66 cents in November. It was steady at that rate until the outbreak of war.

The 1938 devaluation was not consummated by a revaluation of the gold reserves of the Bank of France until November, 1938. The franc was then valued on the market at about 27.6 milligrams of gold, and it was on this basis that the official revaluation was made. The gold reserves in terms of francs were thus raised from 55.8 to 87.2 billions. The difference, more than 30 billion francs, was turned over to the State, which promptly used 23 billions of its new funds to lower its debt to the Bank from 43 to 20 billion francs.[25]

The return of monetary stability.—The formation of the Daladier government and the establishment of the " sterling franc " were accompanied by a welcome return of calm and stability to the Paris money-market. Along with a " spot " position of the franc steady in relation to sterling, the chronic forward discounts against the franc tended to grow smaller, and at the news of the " repli," the forward rates of both sterling and dollars dropped to close to par. Thereafter, the known moderate policies of Daladier and of Marchandeau, his Minister of Finance, helped to maintain the forward discounts on the franc at relatively moderate levels until the Munich crisis. With a reappearance of a drift of capital toward Paris in May,

24 The Daladier decree of May 4, 1938, established only a *lower* limit for the franc (179 per pound sterling) ; there was nothing here to indicate that the franc would not be allowed to appreciate in terms of sterling.

25 *JO, Lois et Décrets,* 1938, pp. 12882-12884.

the *Caisse d'amortissement* found it possible to lower the interest rate on short-term *Bons de la défense nationale* from 4.0 to 2.75 per cent.[26]

The last pre-war panic to trouble the Paris money-market had its origin in the threatening international situation. As tension mounted between Germany and Czechoslovakia in August, 1938, the forward franc again fell to a considerable discount. In spite of repeated assurances of the French government that no bank would be allowed to close its doors, a mild " run " developed. The financial situation was kept in hand by the prompt action of the central bank in discounting all securities and commercial paper offered to it by banks in need of cash, to the value of fifteen billion francs in a few days at the height of the Munich crisis. The total value of bank-notes in circulation rose from 101 to 124 billion francs. With the passing of the panic, total bank-notes in circulation dropped again to about 108 billions,[27] and discounts on forward francs sank to their lowest levels for several years. On the whole, the French banking and monetary system proved remarkably firm during this time of crisis.

The Three Year Plan and the forty-hour week.—After the Munich crisis, the Ministry of Finance in Daladier's administration was given to Paul Reynaud, and France was launched on the " Three Year Plan ": ". . . to lighten the burdens of the Treasury, to free the economy from the obstacles which paralyze its development, to consolidate our money, and finally, by an inflow of investment-seeking capital, to provoke a revival of economic activity." [28]

Thus the Three Year Plan was a step toward " confidence " and away from the socialist program of the Popular Front, following a tendency begun as far back as the Blum " pause " in

26 *Le Temps,* May 16, 1938.

27 *Ibid.,* October 3, 1938.

28 Ministère des Finances, *Le Bilan économique et financier des cinq premiers mois du plan des trois ans* (Paris: Imprimerie Nationale, 1939), p. 1.

February, 1937. The monetary and fiscal policy of this Plan, as announced in the above-quoted program, was to regain the support of the entrepreneurial class through budgetary stability and a stable exchange rate for the franc. " My policy," said Reynaud in his address to the Chamber of Deputies on December 9, 1938, " does not consist of begging for confidence, but in creating facts which motivate confidence, facts which base confidence on realities. . . ." [29]

Reynaud had earlier been one of the first and most steadfast champions of " manipulation " (devaluation) as a solution to France's economic and financial difficulties. But upon assuming the post of minister of finance, he announced that : " The problem of recovery is not a monetary problem; it is an economic, not a financial problem." The era of " monetary manipulations," he declared, was at an end.[30]

Perhaps the most dramatic episode in this change of economic policy was the modification of the forty-hour week, demanded by Reynaud as necessary in order to " unlace the corset in which our country's industry is suffocating." [31] On August 23, 1938, just before the Munich crisis, Daladier had announced his hostility to the forty-hour week, which then became an important symbol for the extreme Left, to be defended at all costs from the encroachments of the conservative government and the capitalists.[32]

The hopes of the French conservatives for changes in the controversial labor laws were realized after the resolution of the Czechoslovakian crisis. In the same series of decree-laws instituting the Three Year Plan were decrees modifying the

29 Paul Reynaud, *Courage de la France* (Paris: Flammarion, 1939), p. 104.

30 *Le Temps,* November 7, 1938.

31 Reynaud, *Sauver le Régime et le Pays* (Paris: Imprimerie Nationale, 1939), pp. 31-32.

32 The forty-hour week was also important as a symbol to the essentially pacifist labor unions because attacks directed against it were often in the name of national defense and the coming war with Germany.

forty-hour week. Although the " legal duration of labor [remained] fixed at forty hours," the working week was extended to six rather than five days, and a simple notification to a Ministry of Labor inspector was enough to extend the work week to forty-eight hours in any enterprise connected with national defense. The government set up a schedule of overtime payments of from 10 to 25 per cent, depending on the total number of overtime hours worked per year.[33]

A united protest from all the labor unions and veterans' organizations met the announcement of this change in the nation's labor policy. In spite of the government's insistence that the country's production had to be increased, a wave of protest strikes began about November 20 and continued even when the government used police and troops to clear out occupied factories. On November 30 a general strike was called; it proved a resounding failure, owing largely to the government's refusal to retreat, and the movement for retention of the " integral " forty-hour week collapsed.[34]

In its struggle with the unions, the government was helped by popular support from those who were gratified by the return of more favorable financial conditions. The government's new monetary policies were apparently achieving a fair degree of success. The years 1938-1939 marked the first sizable immigration of liquid capital since 1936. About fourteen billion sterling francs reentered France in 1938, partly because of recurring rumors of American and British devaluations, and also because wide-spread belief in the imminence of war made French holders of capital anxious to have their funds at hand.[35] The gold reserves at the Bank of France increased by about ten billion francs between the end of 1938 and the end of 1939.

33 *Le Temps*, November 14, 1938.

34 Hourly and daily wage rates remained high. Coal miners' daily wages rose from an average of 50.19 francs in 1937 to 57.91 francs in 1938. The index of hourly wages of skilled workers (*Annuaire Statistique*, 1911 = 100) rose from 807 in 1936 to 1,200 in 1938.

35 *Le Temps financier*, September 19, 1938.

On April 21, 1939, in a radio speech, Reynaud called the franc "the first money of Europe." The Bank of France was able to lower its discount rate to 2 per cent in 1939, and the improved conditions in the Paris money-market made the placing of National Defense securities a comparatively easy undertaking.[36]

PRE-WAR BUSINESS CONDITIONS

In spite of a better atmosphere in financial circles from 1937 to 1939, general business conditions remained unsatisfactory. The discouraging aspect of economic stagnation at a depressed level, familiar to France since 1933, was not changed after the overthrow of the first Popular Front government. At times conditions seemed ripe for a revival, but only the industries benefiting directly from increased armaments production made any impressive gains. In September, 1938 the war scare and mobilization caused a sharp slump in almost all sectors of economic life; this was followed by the best recovery of the decade. But on the whole the approach of war saw French entrepreneurs reluctant to expand their business activities. The low morale, social unrest, and political dissension which characterized France on the eve of the Second World War had their counterparts—if not some of their causes—in the depressed economy of the nation.

Industrial production before the war.—French industry remained depressed throughout the period of rising prices after 1935 and of more stable prices in 1938-1939. Neither the monetary and economic policies of the Popular Front nor those of the more conservative governments which followed seemed to have more than a short-lived beneficial effect on this most important sector of French economic life. The leveling out of wholesale and retail prices after 1938, therefore, was not a result of an improved ratio of goods to money in France.

The last few months of the first Blum administration had been attended by a sharp decline in industrial production. When Chautemps became premier and arranged the devaluation of

36 Pirou, *Cours*, pp. 492-493.

the franc of June 30, 1937, there was a sudden spurt in industrial activity due to buying in anticipation of higher prices, but this soon died out. In August, 1937 the combination of general business depression and the seasonal vacations brought the index of industrial production (1928 = 100) down to 76.1.

In the fall and winter of 1937 the index of industrial production climbed once more, reaching a peak of 91.7 at the end of the year. But this recovery was due to an accidental factor: the Chautemps government had announced a considerable rise in railway freight rates to begin in January, 1938. French industrialists hurried to build up their inventories while transportation costs were still low. As soon as the freight rate increase went into effect, orders fell off, and industrial output shrank once more.[37]

By the end of the Chautemps administration (March, 1938), French industrial production was in another slump. During 1938 the production index slipped almost every month, reaching 70.3 in August, the lowest level of industrial production recorded since the reconstruction years following the First World War. The Munich crisis during the next month completely paralyzed French industry when the partial mobilization removed hundreds of thousands of young laborers from their jobs. But toward the end of 1938, under the stimulus of the obvious approach of war, some branches of French industry made a quick recovery.

During the years 1937-1938 French heavy industries fluctuated on the whole more than did those producing consumers' goods. Pig iron production, for example, showed a marked cyclical variation. After the October, 1936 devaluation of the franc, French pig iron production climbed sharply to a peak at the end of 1937; then, apparently influenced by the world depression, pig iron production fell, reaching a deep trough at the time of the Munich crisis, and rose again steadily to the outbreak of the Second World War.

37 *La France économique en 1938*, pp. 552-553.

The French paper industry, on the other hand, seemed to respond neither to the cyclical upturn in 1936-1937 nor to the depression in the first part of 1938 and, in fact, remained stagnant at depression levels until just before the declaration of war in 1939. The same stagnation was apparent in textiles, leather goods, and the building trades, while the metallurgical and chemical industries acted rather more like pig iron production. The poor showing of consumers' goods industries is partly attributable to the steady loss in purchasing power since 1936 of those groups on fixed incomes.[38] " As a result, the effect of the revival [in 1939] was much less that of enriching the country than of maintaining its level of existence in spite of the increased part devoted to sterile war production." [39]

Balance of trade and payments.—The almost continuous depreciation of the exchange rate of the franc in 1937 and 1938 did not bring any important improvement in the French balance of trade before the end of 1938. In the first nine months of 1937, the value of imports into France increased 72.8 per cent over the same period for 1936. French exports rose also, but their rate of increase was considerably less, despite an exchange depreciation of 25 per cent, which might have been expected to stimulate exports.[40] As a result the deficit in the balance of commodity trade rose from 8.3 billion Poincaré francs in 1936 to 10.0 billions in 1937. In 1938 the balance of trade was improved, but more by the restriction of imports (through the re-imposition of tariff and quota barriers, which the Blum government had lowered slightly) than by improved exports. The quantum index of exports (1927 = 100) rose from 56.1 in 1937 to 60.1 in 1938, while the quantum index of imports fell from 104.0 to 93.0.[41] The con-

38 *L'Activité économique*, 1937, pp. 307-308.

39 Ministère des Finances, *Le Mouvement économique en France de 1929 à 1939* (Paris: Imprimerie Nationale, 1941), p. 144.

40 *L'Activité économique*, 1937, p. 220.

41 League of Nations, *Review of World Trade, 1938* (Geneva, 1939, p. 76.

tinued undervaluation of the French franc due to the devaluations of 1936, 1937, and 1938 was not in itself enough to cause a revival of the French export industry in the years just before the Second World War.

"UNDERVALUATION" AND "OVERVALUATION" OF THE FRANC
IN RELATION TO BRITISH PRICES [42]

May, 1936	145
November, 1936	112
August, 1937	99
February, 1938	92
May, 1938	82
November, 1938	84

In the 1938 balance of current payments, the much lower trade deficit of 6.1 billion Poincaré francs was entirely cancelled out by the tourist trade, freight and insurance charges, and interest and dividends. The revival of general business conditions which marked the last few pre-war months was accompanied by a steady improvement in the French balance of current payments. The trend toward the summer of 1939 was turning in favor of France, so that, but for the outbreak of war, the year 1939 might actually have registered a considerable surplus in the balance of current payments for the first time since 1930.[43]

In 1938 the movements of capital not connected with the exchange of goods and services began to settle down into normal patterns, much to the relief of French financial authorities. The outward-bound tide of French capital was dramatically reversed a few days after Daladier's announcement that the pound sterling would be held at 179 francs. The owners of émigré capital in London responded to this " repli " (May, 1938) by converting eighty million pounds into francs and transferring this immense sum (over fourteen billion francs at

42 The base period is the year 1930; the indexes employed are for the cost of living. A figure over 100 indicates "over-valuation."

43 Ministère des Finances, *Le Mouvement économique en France de 1929 à 1939*, p. 141.

the new rate) back to France within a few days.[44] The British and the French exchange stabilization funds handled this movement of capital so competently that no disturbance resulted in their respective money-markets.[45]

The improved situation in the balance of payments on current account, plus the continued inflow of capital, resulted in a net inflow of gold in 1938 for the first time since 1934. Between October, 1938 and the end of 1939, the combined gold reserves of the Bank and the Fund increased by thirty-seven billion sterling francs.[46] But reduced to 1928 gold equivalents this amounted to only fifteen billion Poincaré francs, less than one-half the amount which had left France since the beginning of 1935.

The achievement of price stability.—A most welcome improvement in French economic life between 1937 and 1939 was the end of the inflationary spiral. The tremendous rise in wholesale prices which had thrown the French business world into disorder in 1936 and 1937 finally slowed down in 1938 and came to a complete halt in 1939—at least until the outbreak of war.

Two of the factors in the stabilization of French wholesale prices during this period were the world depression in the third quarter of 1937 and the fall in world agricultural prices in 1938. The dislocation of the country's economy by the Munich crisis saw a jump in the French index of wholesale food prices, but there was a rapid decline thereafter, partly because of the world-wide decline in food prices, and partly because of the especially good French crops in 1938 and 1939.

A greater emphasis on rearmament during the last peacetime years made for a rather different trend in the wholesale prices of French industrial products. The only drop in the index of this price category was in sympathy with the world

44 Waight, *op. cit.*, p. 111.

45 Because the French Fund absorbed the incoming gold, the statement of the Bank of France shows little increase in its gold reserves at this time.

46 *La France économique de 1939 à 1945*, pp. 1010-1011.

depression at the end of 1937. But this drop was only from 646 in October, 1937 to 626 at the end of the year. Thereafter the rise in wholesale industrial prices was uninterrupted up to the outbreak of war, although the rate of this rise was much slower than that in 1936 and 1937.

TABLE 7

PERCENTAGE CHANGES IN WHOLESALE PRICES, 1937–1939 *

	Foodstuffs	Industrial Products
January, 1936–December, 1936	+ 46.2	+ 54.1
January, 1937–December, 1937	+ 19.2	+ 16.6
January, 1938–December, 1938	+ 8.5	+ 8.2
January, 1939–August, 1939	− 10.5	+ 5.1

* Source: *SGF*. Based on the general index of 126 articles.

The pattern of slower increases in wholesale prices was followed by retail prices and the cost of living. For retail prices a plateau of stability seems to have been achieved by the beginning of 1938, but there was a sharp jump in the last half of the year from an index of 690 to 754.[47] The index of the cost of living compiled by the *SGF*,[48] which had climbed from 80.3 to 99.4 during the first Popular Front government, continued to rise during 1938, but at a much slower rate. Between November, 1937 and November, 1938 the cost of living index rose from 110.0 to 120.3; during the first part of 1939 the cost of living remained stable at this level.

The results of various price control measures enacted by Blum and his successors are most difficult to assess. The first of these measures was a law of August 19, 1936 forbidding "fraudulent" raising of prices of "objects of prime necessity" and establishing national and departmental Committees of Price Surveillance as the guardians of fair prices. The devaluation of June 30, 1937 was immediately followed by an-

47 *SGF,* thirty-four articles, July, 1914 = 100.

48 Working-class family of four, average of all the *départements,* 1930 = 100.

CHART 8.   The Achievement of Price Stability after 1937

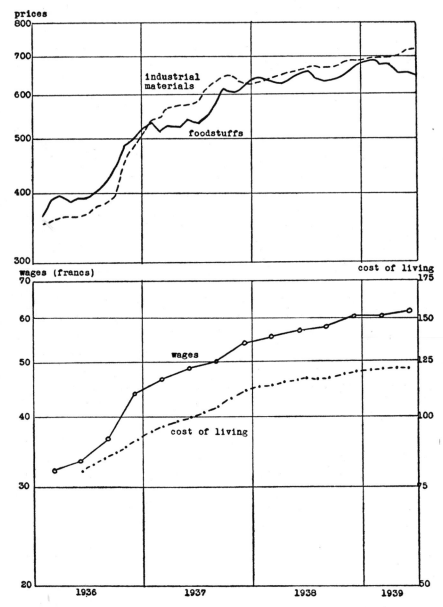

SOURCE: *SGF*. Wages are coal miners' daily wages; for wholesale prices, 1913 = 100; for cost of living, 1930 = 100.

other decree "blocking" prices of wholesale and retail commodities at their June 28, 1937 level. All price increases had to receive prior approval from a Committee of Price Surveillance, except those for agricultural commodities. All agricultural products sold at retail by their producers were exempted from any price control whatsoever.

These measures were modified by decrees of July 28, August 25, and November 5, 1937, which exempted from control all agricultural goods, wholesale and retail, permitted price increases caused by wage increases or exchange fluctuations, and limited those goods subject to control to a specific list published by the National Committee for Price Surveillance. Finally, only specified articles sold at retail were retained on the control list (decree of November 12, 1938). All of these control measures, very diffidently enforced, had almost no effect on France's supremely individualistic farmers, shopkeepers, and industrialists.[49]

The Popular Front price control system, therefore, cannot be regarded as an important factor in contributing to the end of inflation in France. But if the chief factor in slowing down the price rise in the winter of 1937-1938 was the world depression and the fall in agricultural prices, the final stabilization of prices in 1939 is attributable to the end of exchange depreciation. By halting the rising costs of imported materials due to dearer foreign exchange, stabilization of the franc finally snapped the inflationary spiral in France.

The franc and Bank-to-State advances.—Government borrowing from the central bank increased by huge proportions between 1936 and 1938. When the first Popular Front government took office, the only debt of the Treasury to the Bank of France was the 3.2 billion franc "permanent loan" given by the Bank in return for its charter. By the time Blum's first administration was overthrown, an additional seventeen bil-

49 J. Dubergé, *Le Contrôle des prix en France au regard de la théorie économique* (Paris: Librairie Générale de Droit et de Jurisprudence, 1947), p. 33. See aso O. Moreau-Néret, *Le Contrôle des prix en France* (Paris: Recueil Sirey, 1941).

lions had been borrowed from the central bank. Blum's successor, Chautemps, found it necessary to borrow ten billions
more; and at the time of the German occupation of Austria the
total debt of the State to the Bank was raised to forty billion
francs, more than a ten-fold increase in two years.

The Daladier administration managed to steer clear of additional demands on the Bank of France until the time of the
Munich crisis, when an additional ten billion francs was borrowed. But the credit created by the revaluation of the Bank's
gold reserves in November, 1938 presented Daladier with the
opportunity of wiping out over half of the advances.[50] At the
end of 1938 Bank-to-State advances were reduced to 20.6 billions, where they remained until the outbreak of the Second
World War.[51]

As the Treasury borrowed to meet the expenses of government and rearmament and fed the Bank's advances into the
monetary stream, bank-note circulation in France rose at an
ever-increasing rate. All during the depression years the
amount of notes in circulation had remained at eighty-two billion francs or less. The slight business revival in 1936 and the
advances to the Blum government increased this figure to
eighty-five billions; the rise thereafter was more spectacular.
By the end of 1937 there were 91.7 billion francs in bank-
notes; by June, 1938 they had passed the one hundred billion
mark, and by the beginning of the war the total had reached
123 billion francs.

The upward trend of note circulation was not followed by
bank deposits during these years. After the devaluation of
June, 1937 demand deposits at the " Big Four " commercial
banks remained steady at about thirty billion francs, except for

50 Since 1936 the State had gained a total of fifty-four billion francs from
the three devaluations.

51 *Bulletin de Statistique et de Législation comparée.* In November, 1938
the Bank raised its " permanent loan " to the government to ten billion
francs.

the month of the Munich crisis (September, 1938), when they reached thirty-seven billion francs. From the beginning of 1939 until the outbreak of war, demand deposits at the " Big Four " remained at a level of about thirty-four billion francs.

In view of the tremendous rise in prices and the expenses of government, the national debt in France was maintained at a very reasonable level. A large portion of the debt, of course, had been " paid " through revaluation of the Bank of France's gold reserves. By the end of 1936 the total public debt (exclusive of the obligations of the *Caisse d'Amortissement*) stood at 356 billion francs. Between then and December, 1937, the public debt rose to 391 billion francs, and to 413 billions by the end of 1938. Over this two-year period, therefore, the French public debt rose 16 per cent, while wholesale prices rose about 33 per cent. In the month before the outbreak of World War II, the public debt of France stood at 433 billion francs.[52]

Because of the price inflation at this time, the French citizen —who was accustomed to carry enough cash in his wallet to pay his bills—was seriously inconvenienced by the fact that the largest note available was for 1,000 francs. In order to satisfy the need for money of larger denomination, the Bank of France began to circulate notes of 5,000 francs in January, 1938.[53]

With the declaration of war France immediately passed over to a régime of strict control of all monetary institutions. The Office of Exchange Control was set up to handle exchange transactions of currencies and gold. All transfer of gold or other forms of capital from the country by private individuals was forbidden.[54] The Bank of France immediately opened a credit of twenty-five billion francs for the account of the Treasury, and helped private banks meet all requests for the liquidation of deposits. On September 9, 1939 exchange rates were "pegged " for the duration of the war. This act ended the inter-bellum history of the French franc.

52 *Inventaire*, p. 537.

53 Moliexe, *op cit.*, p. 71.

54 *JO, Lois et Décrets*, 1939, pp. 11266-11267.

CHAPTER VII
SUMMARY AND CONCLUSIONS

THE question: "What happened to the French franc between 1919 and 1939?" is a difficult one to answer in any simple or integrated manner. Our study shows that complicated monetary events in France cannot be analyzed apart from institutional, political, and "psychological" elements which often were quite as significant for prices and exchange rates as were more narrowly economic factors. Rather than to try fitting all the data into one body of theoretical propositions, therefore, our method has been to determine which of the monetary developments seemed to have special importance in a given time-span, and then to examine those factors which best explain these developments.

These two decades are crowded with dramatic monetary events. There was hardly a year when some combination of factors was not putting pressure on French prices and exchange rates and calling for changes in French monetary policy.

1919-1922.—The post-war monetary policy of France was based on two unfortunate notions: (1) The expectation that automatically functioning monetary law would sooner or later reëstablish pre-war monetary conditions, including the gold standard, which had been abandoned as a war measure; (2) the hope that the effects of wartime property destruction and currency inflation would be obliterated by German reparations. In the atmosphere of apathy enveloping the nation's political life, basic improvements in the fiscal structure could be avoided. Monetary problems left in the wake of the war could be dismissed with slogans such as " Le Boche paiera! " and measures such as the François-Marsal convention of 1920, which bound the State to repayment of its twenty billion franc debt to the Bank of France in ten annual installments. It was assumed that only this debt stood in the way of complete revalorization of the franc and a return to the gold standard.

196

Deprived of both the gold standard and wartime " pegging " operations, the franc fell to one-third its 1914 exchange value in response to domestic price inflation and the necessity for huge imports of foreign goods for reconstruction. Some of the pressure on the exchange rate of the franc was counterbalanced by the willingness of foreign speculators to buy the depreciated franc in the expectation of an eventual rise to its " true " (purchasing-power-parity) value. The 1920-1921 depression also checked the depreciation of the franc by reducing business activity and the volume of imports.

1923-1926.—The end of the " era of illusions " came with the desperate occupation of the Ruhr, which finally dissipated the " phantom of reparations." A financial panic followed the failure of an important flotation of *Crédit National* bonds. The rate of exchange depreciation assumed ominous proportions, but the legislature and the administration did virtually nothing to protect the franc. The rapid succession of ministries allowed the governments to dodge responsibility while they proclaimed their anguish over the *rentiers'* plight. The legislature, faced with the unpleasant task of raising taxes, expended its energy in useless bickering over whether to " soak the rich " or to increase indirect taxes.

At the beginning of 1924 a speculative " attack on the franc " appeared in several Continental money-markets. This frightening development was temporarily reversed by using the proceeds of a large American-British loan to " squeeze the bears." But after the election victory of the *Cartel des gauches* in the spring of 1924 little vigorous action was taken by either the government or the Bank of France in behalf of the franc. Cut off from the *rentiers'* savings by the loss of confidence, the Treasury had to appeal to the Bank for loans, which were most grudgingly advanced. Tension between the *Cartel* and the " mur d'argent " revealed itself in the astonishing incidents when, as we have seen, the Herriot ministries were overthrown with the help of the governor of the Bank of France.

Not all Frenchmen were hurt by the monetary crisis; besides the speculators, entrepreneurs associated with the tourist and export trades benefited from the depreciating value of the franc. In general, these years of monetary weakness were prosperous ones for the business community. Thanks partly to the reconstruction effort, France enjoyed full employment and a volume of industrial production which surpassed that of pre-war years.

Because of the existence of full employment the capital flight was translated into an increasing pressure on French prices. In response to the outflow of capital, the exchange rate depreciated so rapidly that the franc became considerably undervalued. The rising volume of exports which resulted from the relative cheapness of French goods drove up prices by adding to national money income on the one hand, and by depriving France of a larger fraction of domestic production on the other.

When it became apparent to all that the government was incapable of taking effective action, bearish speculative pressure was aggravated by an " increase in money conciousness " on the part of the ordinary citizen. Shopkeepers turned " amateur cambist " by adjusting their prices to daily foreign exchange quotations, and *rentiers* sold their *bons* for diamonds. Domestic prices, therefore, developed a dangerous tendency to fluctuate in coordination with the exchange rate of the franc. During this, the runaway phase of the French inflation, the influence of *rentier* and speculative expectations was exerted directly on exchange rates and prices, by-passing the ordinary relationships of money and commerce. All France was in " flight from the franc " in 1925-1926, one of those periods when, as Keynes puts it, "enterprise becomes the bubble on the whirlpool of inflation."

1926-1928.—Confronted by a " National Union " government under Poincaré, the monetary crisis suddenly evaporated. The speculators evidently believed that, given a trustworthy administration, they had pushed the franc too far. Emigré capital reëntered France in a rush, providing the Bank of

France with a large reserve of gold and foreign exchange as a basis for a return to the gold standard. Encouraged by Poincaré's gestures in the direction of restoring confidence, the rentiers resumed their purchases of government securities.

At the end of 1926 a " *de facto* stabilization " of the franc was established through the operations of the Bank of France on the foreign exchange market. Now the speculative trend was reversed, and to avoid an appreciation of the franc from its 1927 level the banks and export industries pressed the government to place the franc solidly on a gold standard. In spite of Poincaré's hopes for a complete revalorization of the franc in the interests of the *rentiers,* the " *de jure* stabilization " (devaluation) was accomplished in June, 1928, when the new franc was launched with one-fifth the gold content of the *Germinal* franc.

1929-1932.—The success of the Poincaré franc was apparently complete. Capital which had left during the " flight from the franc " continued to flow back into France, and was soon joined by " hot money " in refuge from the impending devaluations of the pound sterling and the dollar. The gold reserves of the Bank of France grew by phenomenal proportions, to the distress of economists and financiers (outside of France) who were concerned over this " maldistribution " of the world's gold stocks.

At the same time the French economy was exhibiting a curious resistance to the first stages of the Great Depression. Industrial production remained high through 1930, and there were many other indications of prosperity—high wages, full employment, and, especially, a spectacular rise in agricultural prices. Proponents of the quantity theory of money were quick to seize upon the presence of both a large volume of money and good times in France as proof of their theories.

But a large amount of the money which had recently arrived in France represented capital which was not invested in the economy; instead, it was hoarded or placed in savings banks which did not use their assets for commercial loans. A more meaningful approach to the lag in the depression is to consider those factors which made for high national income at this time. According to this view, the chief contribution of large volumes of capital was to keep money easy and to prevent financial panics and credit constriction such as had marked the beginning of the depression elsewhere. France also benefited from the fact that her exports were predominantly consumers' goods and services, while the depression affected first the capital-goods industries. Much more important was the relationship of international payments to French income. All through the 1920's, France had had a large surplus in the balance of payments on current account. The devaluation of 1928 fixed the franc at an undervalued rate, which tended to perpetuate the disequilibrium and the current surpluses. The delayed " multiplier " effects of these surpluses made for a relatively high level of French national income in 1930 and 1931, even though the trade disequilibrium was disappearing as international commerce contracted and French goods became increasingly dear.

While it lasted, France's Golden Glow inspired her authorities and business leaders with a false sense of security. They were convinced that the flood of gold toward France was the result of the superiority of the nation's monetary and financial system. The problems besetting France—the depression and the end of reparations—" came from the outside." The Treasury had accumulated large revenue surpluses which wiped out the budgetary deficits of 1930 and 1931 and even allowed a slight reduction of the national debt and of taxation. The legislature had been encouraged thereupon to raise governmental expenditures, in spite of vehement warnings from the financial purists. But when the full weight of the depression did come home to France, and Treasury surpluses turned into deficits, the country surrendered to the proponents of deliberate deflation.

1933-1935.—Now French price levels and the cost of living began to decline at an alarming rate, while prices in most other countries were recovering. Reversing the situation of the years 1929-1932, agricultural products were the victims of the worst price slump in France, in spite of the ever-increasing protection they enjoyed from foreign competition. Farmers were powerless to restrict the yield of their especially large crops during these years, while the industrialists, protected by newly-established quotas against foreign products, did cut their output. The prices of industrial products, therefore, were steady— though at a depressed level.

The devaluation of the American dollar, following the devaluation of the pound, had made the franc much more valuable in gold and foreign currency than in terms of its internal purchasing power. On the one hand, this deprived France of many of her former markets; on the other, by cheapening foreign prices in terms of francs and reducing the cost of imports, these devaluations added to the depressive influences on French price levels.

To the dismay of monetary authorities, even the huge volume of gold at the Bank of France was not proof against the speculation for a fall in the franc which now developed. In addition to the drain of gold resulting from the outward flow of capital, a deficit appeared in the balance of payments, necessitating further shipments of gold from the country. The exchange rate remained stable, but only at the price of a serious level of unemployment and the loss of one-third of the Bank's gold reserves. On the forward exchange market, frightening discounts against the franc appeared with each panic, especially after the February riots in 1934 and the Belgian devaluation in 1935.

For the French authorities, whose attention was rigidly fixed on financial rather than economic developments, the only possible course of action was to " save the franc "—that is, to save the gold standard and to spare the *rentiers* from another devaluation. Reasoning that Poincaré's success had been due to his successful termination of budgetary deficits, they hoped that the same tactics would convince speculators once again that the franc was unassailable.

As the depression wore on, this almost instinctive reëmphasis on the gold standard and on tried and true methods of public finance gradually was elaborated into a full-blown theory of curtailment of government expenditures as a monetary policy. Budgetary stability was regarded as the only means of protecting the country from the sort of financial panic that had caused so much grief in London and New York. Another favorite argument was that budgetary retrenchment would actually *increase* national income, by reducing that part of it devoted to "sterile" public expenditures. The legislature surrendered its control over financial affairs, giving the administration power to enact stiff doses of retrenchment by decree.

By 1934 the overvaluation of the franc was strangling the export trades. To solve this dilemma without recourse to devaluation, the deflationists enlarged the scope of their theory: they argued that, rather than slice away another portion of the bond-holders' savings, the country must force down prices and wages, which would lower the costs of production and enable French goods to compete in foreign markets once more.

When *rentier* as well as speculator became convinced that a devaluation was in the offing, the movement of capital out of France was greatly speeded up. A huge volume of hoarded bank-notes suddenly converged on the Bank for exchange against gold. The British Exchange Equalisation Account was hard pressed to absorb the French capital which came flooding into London. A great deal of "hot money" from France and the other gold bloc countries also found its way to New York. The same loss of confidence which sent gold streaming out of the country made for a decline in the volume of government short-term securities outstanding; at the same time the government's income from taxes was falling off, and, in spite of heroic efforts, expenditures remained virtually incompressible. As a result the government was forced to attempt secret arrangements with the Bank for loans via the medium of discounting Treasury *bons*. The administration did not dare to fall back on the dreaded expedient of Bank-to-State advances. As a favor to Laval and in order to support deflationist policies, the Bank complied.

But the deflationary experiments were failures in all of their aims. Not even the lowering of French price levels can be attributed to them, since only agricultural prices fell by any considerable amounts after 1933, and farm commodities were exempted for the most part from deflationary edicts. Government expenditures were cut; due to lower tax receipts, however, deficits remained large and the national debt continued to rise. The amount of reduction in expenditures was slight, as it has to be in a modern state with manifold responsibilities and a heavy debt service. The worst mistake of the deflationists was in thinking that entrepreneurs would be encouraged by lowered costs, when what was really needed as incentives were higher profits. It is perhaps fortunate for France that her financial authorities at this time were not completely successful in their attempts to correct the overvaluation of the franc by internal price deflation; this would have resulted in a reduction of the French price structure of about 35 per cent from its already depressed level.

1936-1937.—Riding into office on the crest of a revulsion against the tactics of the deflationists, the Popular Front first experimented with " reflation." Taking his cue from the New Deal, Blum sought to raise the purchasing power of the lower classes and to end the depression by shortening the work week, promoting collective bargaining contracts, financing huge public works, and raising the prices of agricultural products. Only a few changes were made in the tax structure; it was assumed that a satisfactory fiscal situation would automatically result from a revivified economy.

When the hoped-for recovery did not appear by September, 1936, Blum suddenly announced an " alignment " of the franc. The Poincaré franc, which had been set at 65.5 milligrams of gold, was replaced by the Auriol " elastic " franc with limits of

49 and 43 milligrams of gold, and the Bank was allowed to suspend gold convertibility. Free trade in gold was abolished, and a new institution, the Exchange Stabilization Fund, was given the task of controlling exchange fluctuations.

But after the widespread application of the forty-hour week, the slight business recovery which had followed the devaluation quickly disappeared, and the franc became the object of a speculative attack which cost the Fund all of its reserves. Forced to recognize the importance of financial stability and "confidence," Blum ordered a "pause" in the reform movement to "digest" those social advances already in force. The Fund was placed in the hands of experts trusted in business circles, and the Auriol franc was allowed to slip to its lower gold-equivalent limit in an attempt to find its "natural" level.

In spite of the government's more conservative policies, the speculative attack continued. When free trade in gold (but not convertibility) was restored, gold once again joined the outward movement of "hot money." In spite of the huge volume of bank-notes injected into the economy by the government, total note circulation remained stable because the Fund had to absorb such vast amounts of short-term capital seeking refuge in foreign currencies.

Since the output of goods remained depressed while prices and the cost of living soared, the effect of the Popular Front was not to raise the real national income of France, but to cause drastic shifts in the distribution of that income. The monetary benefits accruing to organized labor from paid holidays, contract settlements, and arbitration awards were wiped out by the rising cost of living; the forty-hour week, however, did bring a considerable reduction in unemployment. Those classes on fixed incomes suffered the brunt of the inflation. The entrepreneurial classes, which could profit from rising prices, were, paradoxically, the chief beneficiaries of the Blum experiments.

But rising profits were not enough to stimulate a genuine business recovery in France at this time. The supply of labor, especially skilled labor, was cut too deeply by the sudden establishment of the forty-hour week. And deep distrust of Popular Front policies kept the industrialists from inaugurating any noteworthy expansion. After nine months in power, Blum embarked on appeasement of French financial circles in order to end the monetary crisis and to ease the pressure on the Treasury. As part of this appeasement, he was forced to gamble on a stable exchange rate; this sealed the fate of his government. The financial circles which controlled the exchange market were among his bitterest enemies.

1937-1939.—Although the Popular Front governments which followed Blum's régime continued to show a conciliatory attitude toward capitalism, the entrepreneurial class refused to cooperate. The violent attacks on the exchange rate of the franc continued, and were aggravated by the crisis resulting from the shaky international situation in 1937. The devaluation of June 30, 1937 eased the monetary situation only fleetingly, and the exodus of French capital soon was resumed.

But in April, 1938 the control of the French government by the Popular Front ended. Daladier devalued the franc once more and adopted a sterling exchange standard. The pressure on the franc slowly evaporated, in spite of the panic produced by the Munich war scare. Confidence in the government's ability to maintain the sterling franc was aided by the modification of the controversial forty-hour week and the inauguration of Reynaud's " Three Year Plan " to end financial instability and to enlarge French industrial output. A reflux of émigré capital helped calm the Parisian money-market.

In spite of the success of the Daladier régime in the financial arena, industrial production and general business conditions remained in a slump until just before the outbreak of the Second World War. And although the three devaluations of the franc since September, 1936 had kept the franc " undervalued " in respect to other currencies, export trades were still depressed.

The most notable economic achievement of the post-Popular Front administrations was in stopping the price inflation which had been undermining the nation's economic life since June, 1936. The price control measures instituted by Blum and his successors had proved virtually ineffective, and they were now modified out of existence. Three factors helped to snap the inflationary spiral in France: the world depression of 1937-1938, the fall in world and French agricultural prices in 1938 and 1939, and—perhaps most significant of all—the end of exchange depreciation which had been raising the prices of commodities imported into France.

.   .   .   .

At any given time in the period under study, prices and exchange rates in France were determined by a complex interplay of many factors, none of which dominated the whole interbellum history of the franc. At certain stages, cyclical fluctuations in the national economy (including changes in national income, employment, and investment) seemed most important. But these factors could never be considered apart from the balance of international payments, the quantity and velocity of money in circulation, and the status of the French fisc; each of these, at one time or another, seemed to play a preponderant role in monetary developments. It would be difficult indeed to reduce the monetary history of France from 1919 to 1939 to any formula or set of formulas.

All the above factors came into play along with other less narrowly economic influences. Chief among these were the institutional framework (the monetary agencies, customs of the money-market, and the sort of monetary standard employed), the monetary and economic policies in vogue, and the " level of confidence " (*rentier,* entrepreneurial, and speculative expectations).

A sudden change in any of these factors produced a threat to the stability of prices and exchange rates. If appropriate offsetting measures were not taken by the State, additional factors were likely to converge in a mutually aggravating crisis, producing violent attacks on the exchange position of the currency (as in 1925-1926 and in 1935-1936) and vicious spirals of inflation (as in 1924-1926 and 1936-1938). At such times prices and exchange rates broke away from their usual connections with industry and trade; under the pressure of a sudden loss of confidence, all the monetary factors began to change rapidly and in close coordination. French monetary crises, therefore, involved a multiplicity of forces which gathered momentum and weight like a landslide.

In their attempts to deal with deteriorating monetary situations the authorities of France were handicapped by the prejudices of her citizens. The notion of managing their currency was repugnant to Frenchmen who, along with their faith in the "automatic" gold standard, doubted the advisability of allowing bureaucrats to rush in where the mightiest "expert" feared to tread.

In all of France's monetary difficulties, from the time of Poincaré to the time of Reynaud, the French government was forced to take the position that its duty was limited to correcting the malfunctioning of an essentially sound system. Each great effort—stabilization by Poincaré, deflation by Laval, "reflation" by Blum—was presented as an adjustment needed to repair the machinery of self-regulating monetary laws. Each reduction in the exchange rate of the franc was undertaken as a method of last resort, and was regarded as a "devaluation to end devaluations." That is why so many of the policies were expressed in defensive terms: "to stop hostile speculation"; "to end loss of confidence"; "to correct the unbalanced budget"; "to end the overvaluation of the franc"; "to stop the gold hemorrhage"; "to save the franc."

Stubborn faith in the automatic functioning of monetary laws was one of the reasons why, for seven years following the First World War, virtually nothing was done to stop the headlong depreciation of the franc. The government, the people, and even professional speculators expected the *Germinal* franc to reappear as it had after abandonment of the gold standard in the crisis years 1848 and 1870. Finally the Poincaré administration stepped in, produced a midget replica of the nineteenth-century gold franc, and stepped back again with a sigh of relief. But the precedent for " monetary manipulations " by the State had been set.

When the currency was threatened once more, this time by the Great Depression, the country again turned to the State. Ironically enough, the governments of Doumergue and Laval had to flout many other tenets of laissez-faire economics in attempting to preserve one—the gold franc: the deflationary decree-laws represented an extensive interference in the economic life of the nation.

Under the Popular Front several elements of currency control were added: greater authority over the central bank; the Exchange Stabilization Fund; the end of gold convertibility; some embryonic price-control bodies; the Bond Defense Fund; and " open-market " facilities for the Bank of France comparable to those of the British and American central banks. But even Blum refused to demolish that last bastion of monetary liberty, the free foreign exchange market. Even the leaders of the Socialist party shared in the belief that there was a connection between political freedom and lack of monetary restraints. The Laval and Blum policies, different in so many respects, were alike in that both devaluation and deflation were attempts to lower prices in terms of gold *within* the existing system of liberal institutions.

In spite of the wishes of the French public and French authorities, the trend was toward a managed currency. By the end of 1937 the government had become accustomed to asking for *pleins-pouvoirs* to deal with almost every fiscal and monetary contingency. The governments which were able to restore financial confidence in the 1930's (Laval in 1935, Daladier-Reynaud in 1938) certainly did not achieve their success by abandoning controls over the monetary mechanism. In fact, the locus of public confidence shifted from the presence or absence of "monetary manipulation" to the economic and financial ideology of the government in power.

The French desire for a stable, unregulated currency remains unsatisfied today. As a result, while some economists have shifted their attention to concepts such as national income and long-range planning for maximum production, the "old guard" is still fighting the thirty-year-old battle for stable money.

APPENDIXES AND BIBLIOGRAPHICAL NOTES

APPENDIX I

FRANCS PER DOLLAR IN PARIS

	Jan.	Feb.	March	April	May	June	July	Aug.	Sept.	Oct.	Nov.	Dec.
1919	5.45	5.45	5.76	5.98	6.35	6.38	6.87	7.74	8.38	8.60	9.30	10.87
1920	12.08	14.07	14.00	15.91	14.56	12.42	12.37	13.82	14.96	15.35	16.68	16.80
1921	15.46	13.94	14.14	13.61	12.12	12.40	12.80	12.94	13.54	13.88	14.03	13.14
1922	12.28	11.48	11.16	10.90	10.99	11.51	12.29	12.66	12.98	13.58	14.62	13.84
1923	14.98	16.28	15.94	15.01	15.06	15.88	16.97	17.69	17.14	16.80	18.22	19.02
1924	21.42	22.65	21.68	16.37	17.35	19.11	19.57	18.36	18.85	19.12	18.96	18.51
1925	18.54	18.94	19.28	19.26	19.38	20.98	21.30	21.32	21.22	22.54	25.32	26.74
1926	26.52	27.23	27.95	29.56	31.93	34.12	40.96	35.42	35.05	34.15	29.12	25.33
1927	25.26	25.48	25.55	25.53	25.53	25.54	25.55	25.51	25.50	25.47	25.45	25.40
1928	25.44	25.44	25.41	25.40	25.40	25.44	25.53	25.59	25.60	25.60	25.60	25.57
1929	25.59	25.60	25.60	25.59	25.59	25.57	25.53	25.55	25.55	25.43	25.39	25.39
1930	25.44	25.53	25.55	25.51	25.49	25.48	25.41	25.41	25.46	25.48	25.46	25.44
1931	25.50	25.50	25.55	25.57	25.56	25.54	25.50	25.51	25.47	25.39	25.51	25.49
1932	25.44	25.38	25.42	25.36	25.33	25.40	25.50	25.52	25.52	25.47	25.52	25.62
1933	25.62	25.49	25.40	24.36	21.70	20.77	18.25	18.62	17.23	17.13	15.97	16.31
1934	16.06	15.49	15.19	15.11	15.12	15.15	15.16	15.01	14.98	15.09	15.18	15.16
1935	15.19	15.17	15.10	15.15	15.18	15.13	15.09	15.09	15.17	15.18	15.18	15.16
1936	15.10	14.97	15.07	15.17	15.18	15.17	15.10	15.18	15.19	21.47	21.51	21.42
1937	21.42	21.48	21.73	22.25	22.34	22.46	26.26	26.66	28.36	29.85	29.44	29.45
1938	29.92	30.49	32.06	32.23	35.47	35.94	36.13	36.57	37.17	37.51	37.95	37.99
1939	37.92	37.77	37.74	37.76	37.75	37.74						

Source: *SGF*. January, 1919–September, 1922—average of daily quotations; October, 1922–June, 1939—average of high and low for the month; of daily quotations.

APPENDIX II

Estimates of National Income in France

Before the recent war, no satisfactory statistics of French national income were to be found. It was not until after the Liberation that French economists began to pursue the fruitful line of research represented by studies in national income. Until then the estimates of L. Dugé de Bernonville, published in the *Revue d' économie politique,* were most often employed. But these estimates, which were really estimates of personal income (*revenus privés*), tended to be gross underestimations of French national income. The primary cause of this underestimation lay in the fact that Dugé de Bernonville had to use tax returns as the basis for his estimates; as everyone knows, the art of avoiding tax payments is brought to a high peak of perfection in France. Dugé de Bernonville himself refused to correct his national income estimates for price changes or to employ them as anything but an indication of trend.[1]

Following are Dugé de Bernonville's estimates in billions of current francs:

1913	*36*	1929	245
1920	110	1930	243
1921	115	1931	229
1922	119	1932	206
1923	134	1933	199
1924	155	1934	184
1925	172	1935	175
1926	208	1936	201
1927	210	1937	242
1928	227	1938	267

In his *Conditions of Economic Progress,*[2] Colin Clark attempts to correct for the discrepancy in Dugé de Bernonville's estimates by adding to them French tax returns. The pro-

1 *La France économique en 1936,* pp. 549-550.

2 New York: Macmillan Co., 1940.

cedure is highly questionable, since salaries of government employees thus are counted twice. Even so, Clark's results (corrected for price changes on the basis of 1925-1934 average prices) still are lower than the most recent estimates:

1920	180	1928	259
1921	211	1929	245
1922	228	1930	240
1923	227	1931	244
1924	238	1932	226
1925	247	1933	229
1926	246	1934	217
1927	247		

Recently a number of French economists, including Alfred Sauvy (Institut de Conjoncture), François Perroux and others connected with the Institut de science économique appliquée, and a group of young economists at the Commissariat Général du Plan ("Monnet Plan") have turned their earnest attention to the techniques of "comptabilité nationale." While most of their work is directed, of course, to the years since the war, a few attempts at retrospective studies have been made. For the year 1938, at least, we possess an estimate of national income and national product which seems somewhat comparable in validity to national income estimates in England and the United States. The techniques and categories employed, at any rate, are similar to those of the Scandinavian and Anglo-Saxon economists; on the other hand, the statistics on which these estimates must be based still suffer from the stubborn reluctance of the French to divulge information.

Among the recent French studies of national income is that issued under the auspices of the Commissariat Général du Plan, *Estimation du revenu national français* (Paris: Imprimerie Nationale, 1947), which is the work of R. Froment and J. Dumontier. In addition to an estimate of the national income in 1938, these economists have included "projections" for 1946, 1947, and 1950 for the level of income needed for successful fulfillment of the goals of the Monnet Plan.

(billions of 1938 francs)

1938	1946	1947	1950	
328	264	291	435	private production income at factor costs
35	28	38	46	indirect taxes
− 8	− 11	− 5	...	subsidies
355	281	324	481	private production income at market prices
20	31	28	23	government services
375	312	352	504	net national product

The aggregates of national income employed by the United States Department of Commerce are rather different from those used by the French. For the purpose of conforming to American terminology, the above statistics may be re-assembled as follows:

(billions of 1938 francs)

1938	1946	1947	1950	
328	264	291	435	private production income at factor costs
20	31	28	23	government services
348	295	319	458	national income
− 8	− 11	− 5	...	subsidies
35	28	38	46	indirect taxes
375	312	352	504	net national product

Working backward from the estimate for 1938, Froment and P. Gavanier have constructed estimates for the inter-war period of private production income at factor costs.[3] While the results are extremely rough approximations, they are probably the best estimates yet available for the years under consideration.

3 *La France économique, 1939-1945*, p. 928. The authors acknowledge that these figures (aside from those for 1938) have a range of error of ± 20 per cent.

PRIVATE PRODUCTION INCOME

(billions of 1938 francs)

1920	233	1930	386
1921	216	1931	369
1922	262	1932	344
1923	283	1933	345
1924	329	1934	338
1925	331	1935	324
1926	346	1936	320
1927	334	1937	331
1928	354	1938	328
1929	391	1939	351

APPENDIX III

BALANCES OF PAYMENTS
(billions of 1928 francs)

(−: payments to foreigners; no sign: payments from foreigners)

Year	Balance of Commodity Trade	Tourist Items, Insurance, Freight, Remittances	Interest and Dividends	Service of Inter-Allied Debts	Reparations	Balance of Payments on Current Account	Ditto, Minus Reparations and Allied Debts*	Gold Movements	Known Capital Movements (incl. Govt. and B. of F.)	Presumed "Invisible" Capital Movements and Errors — Inflow	Outflow
1920	−35.9	9.2	−1.0		3.0	−24.7	−27.7	.8	−4.3	28.2	...
1921	−.4	7.2	2.0		.9	9.7	8.8	.4	−2.8	...	7.3
1922	−4.9	8.0	2.4		1.4	6.9	5.5	.1	−1.5	...	8.3
1923	−4.8	7.7	1.8			4.7	4.7	−.3	−5.0	...	...
1924	.4	6.9	2.9		3.3	13.5	10.2	.3		...	11.1
1925	−1.6	10.7	−.8		3.0	11.3	8.3	.2	−2.6	...	11.3
1926	−2.0	11.3			3.1	12.4	9.3	...	−.8	...	13.2
1927	.1	7.3	2.2	−1.5	4.2	12.3	9.6	.5	−23.1	10.6	...
1928	−3.3	9.0	3.2	−1.8	5.5	12.6	8.9	−6.5	−9.7	3.6	...
1929	−11.1	9.6	5.0	−2.1	6.7	8.1	3.5	−8.6	−2.0	2.5	...
1930	−12.9	9.1	4.7	−2.8	7.1	5.2	.9	−11.7	−2.7	9.2	...
1931	−13.2	6.9	3.4	−1.3	2.6	−1.6	−2.9	−18.5	−8.3	28.4	...
1932	−10.1	4.0	1.2			−4.9		−18.5	21.0	2.4	...
1933	−9.0	4.3	1.8			−2.9		2.1	2.5	...	1.7
1934	−6.7	3.1	2.5			−1.1		−1.5	.3	2.3	...
1935	−6.0	1.6	3.6			−.8		14.9	1.8	...	15.9
1936	−8.3	1.6	3.8			−2.9		20.6	.3	...	18.0
1937	−10.0	2.1	3.9			−4.0		6.5	2.2	...	4.7
1938	−6.1	2.8	3.5			.2		−3.0	.3	2.5	...

Source: League of Nations, *Balances of Payments* (Geneva; 1938), p. 53. "Presumed 'Invisible' Capital Movements and Errors" is a balancing item, included only to demonstrate the trend. These figures differ slightly from the estimates of "invisible" capital movements given annually in *La France économique* because revised estimates were published in the 1938 League of Nations volume, and because for some items in this Appendix it was necessary to use the estimates from *L'Evolution de l'Economie française*, Table 19.

*Minus reparations only in the period 1920–1926.

APPENDIX IV

Government Head	Took Office	Minister of Finance *	Took Office
Viviani	June 13, 1914	Noulens	June 13, 1914
Viviani	Aug. 26, 1914	Ribot	Aug. 26, 1914
Briand	Oct. 29, 1915		
Briand	Dec. 12, 1916		
Ribot	Mar. 20, 1917	Thierry	Mar. 20, 1917
Painlevé	Sept. 12, 1917	Klotz	Sept. 12, 1917
Painlevé	Oct. 23, 1917		
Clemenceau	Nov. 16, 1917		
Millerand	Jan. 20, 1920	François-Marsal	Jan. 20, 1920
Briand	Jan. 16, 1921	Doumer	Jan. 16, 1921
Poincaré	Jan. 14, 1922	de Lasteyrie	Jan. 15, 1922
Poincaré	Mar. 28, 1924	François-Marsal	Mar. 30, 1924
François-Marsal	June 8, 1924		
Herriot	June 14, 1924	Clémentel	June 14, 1924
		De Monzie	April 3, 1925
Painlevé	April 17, 1925	Caillaux	April 17, 1925
		⎧ Painlevé	Oct. 29, 1925
Painlevé	Oct. 29, 1925	⎨ Georges Bonnet	
		⎩ (Budget)	"
Briand	Nov. 25, 1925	Loucheur	Nov. 29, 1925
		Doumer	Dec. 17, 1925
Briand	Mar. 9, 1926	Peret	Mar. 10, 1926
Briand	June 23, 1926	Caillaux	June 24, 1926
Herriot	July 19, 1926	De Monzie	July 20, 1926
Poincaré	July 23, 1926	Poincaré	July 24, 1926
Poincaré	Nov. 11, 1928	Chéron	Nov. 12, 1928
Briand	July 29, 1929		
Tardieu	Nov. 3, 1929		
Chautemps	Feb. 21, 1930	⎰ Dumont	Feb. 22, 1930
		⎱ Palmade (Budget)	"
		⎧ Reynaud	Mar. 3, 1930
Tardieu	Mar. 2, 1930	⎨ Germain-Martin	
		⎩ (Budget)	"
Steeg	Dec. 13, 1930	⎰ Germain-Martin	Dec. 14, 1930
		⎱ Palmade (Budget)	"
Laval	Jan. 26, 1931	⎰ Flandin	Jan. 28, 1931
		⎱ Piétri (Budget)	"
Laval	June 13, 1931		
Laval	Jan. 12, 1932		

GOVERNMENT HEADS AND MINISTERS OF FINANCE (*Continued*)

Government Head	Took Office	Minister of Finance *	Took Office
Tardieu	Feb. 21, 1932	Flandin	Feb. 21, 1932
Herriot	June 4, 1932	{ Germain-Martin { Palmade (Budget)	June 4, 1932 "
Paul-Boncour	Dec. 18, 1932	Chéron	Dec. 18, 1932
Daladier	Jan. 31, 1933	{ Georges Bonnet { Lamoureux (Budget)	Jan. 31, 1933 "
Sarraut	Oct. 26, 1933	{ Georges Bonnet { Gardey (Budget)	Oct. 26, 1933 "
Chautemps	Nov. 26, 1933	{ Georges Bonnet { Marchandeau (Budget)	Nov. 27, 1933 "
Daladier	Jan. 30, 1934	Piétri	Jan. 30, 1934
		Marchandeau	Feb. 4, 1934
Doumergue	Feb. 9, 1934	Germain-Martin	Feb. 9, 1934
Flandin	Nov. 9, 1934		
Buisson	June 1, 1935		
Laval	June 7, 1935	Régnier	June 8, 1935
Sarraut	Jan. 24, 1936		
Blum	June 4, 1936	Auriol	June 5, 1936
Chautemps	June 22, 1937	Georges Bonnet	June 22, 1937
Chautemps	Jan. 18, 1938	Marchandeau	Jan. 18, 1938
Blum	Mar. 13, 1938	{ Blum (Treasury) { Spinasse (Budget)	Mar. 13, 1938 "
Daladier	April 10, 1938	Marchandeau	April 10, 1938
		Reynaud	Nov. 1, 1938

* At times there was a special minister in charge of the budget (and in March, 1938 Blum was his own " Minister of the Treasury "); these are indicated in addition to the Ministers of Finance in the same administration.

BIBLIOGRAPHICAL NOTES

Reference Works

The basic French reference for recent statistical material is the *Bulletin de la Statistique générale de la France et du Service d'observation des prix* (Paris: Félix Alcan), a quarterly containing the official statistics pertaining to population, agriculture, commerce, industry, and finance. The *SGF* also publishes articles by outstanding French statisticians, economists, and demographers. Just as authoritative but limited to financial statistics is the Ministry of Finance's *Bulletin de Statistique et de législation comparée* (Paris: Imprimerie Nationale), which includes the weekly Bank of France statements. Some of the data in the above-cited works can be found in handy form for comparison over the years in the *Annuaire Statistique*, prepared by the Institut national de la statistique et des études économiques (Paris: Imprimerie Nationale) and in the huge *Inventaire de la situation financière (1913-1946)* (Paris: Imprimerie Nationale, 1946) published under the direction of Robert Schuman for legislators trying to cope with the wreckage of France's post-war fiscal structure. In addition to charts and tables, the last-named work contains Schuman's appraisal of France's post-Liberation financial problems.

One of the best sources for French economic history since the First World War is *La France économique*, an annual review of national economic life by experts in several fields, published by the *Revue d'économie politique*. Of special interest is the enlarged number *De la France d'avant-guerre à la France d'aujourd'hui* (*Revue d'économie politique*, Vol. 53, January-February, 1939), surveying the years 1911-1936. Publication of this series was suspended during the recent war, but *La France économique* reappeared in 1947 in two large numbers covering the years 1939-1945 (Vol. 57, September-October and November-December, 1947). The Institut scientifique de Recherches économiques et sociales has published an impressive collection of statistical tables called *L'Evolution de l'économie française, 1910-1937* (Paris: Recueil Sirey, 1937). Between 1935 and 1939 a quarterly summary of economic and financial conditions in France called *L'Activité économique* was published jointly by the Institut de statistique de l'Université de Paris and the Institut scientifique de Recherches économiques et sociales.

The numerous publications of the League of Nations contain a wealth of information on economic and financial developments. The series, *Statistical Yearbook, World Production and Prices, Money and Banking, Balances of Payments* (especially that for 1938), and *Review of World Trade*, can be used to compare economic developments in France in various periods with those of the world. Many of the important French economic and financial time series, some of which have been corrected for seasonal fluctuations, can be examined in the files of the National Bureau of Economic Research in New York City.

The Institut de science économique appliquée in Paris has a mimeographed *Chronologie monétaire* of landmarks in monetary history in France and abroad; this is more complete for the period 1914-1928 than for the second inter-bellum decade. The *SGF* lists the exchange rates of the principal currencies at Paris, but for forward exchange one must resort to the unpublished *Cours des changes* at the Bank of France or the rather inexact observations in *Le Temps*. The rate of the franc in New York, as well as the standing of the Bank of France, is carried in the *Federal Reserve Bulletin*, published by the Board of Governors of the Federal Reserve System.

Some idea as to how the French reacted to the spectacular monetary events of these years can be obtained from legislative debates on financial questions in the *Journal Officiel*, which also contains laws, decrees, and committee reports. Among the French newspapers of the period, that most concerned with financial matters was *Le Temps*, which also carried weekly supplements called *Le Temps économique et financier* or *Le Temps financier*, especially valuable for the articles of Frédéric Jenny, which reflected the conservative attitudes of French business and banking circles. The viewpoint of the Bank of France officials can be seen in the *Compte rendu* (Paris: Dupont), their annual report to the stockholders.

MONOGRAPHS AND ARTICLES

On French economic conditions.—An invaluable guide to studies in the modern history of France is Shepard B. Clough, *France, A History of National Economics, 1789-1939* (New York: Charles Scribner's Sons, 1939). Recent developments in French business conditions are surveyed and the weaknesses of the French economy are analyzed from the conservative point of view in Robert Wolff, *Economie et finances de la France, passé et avenir* (New York: Brentano's, 1943), and from the Marxist point of view in Charles Bettelheim, *Bilan de l'économie française, 1919-1946* (Paris: Presses Universitaires, 1947). See also C.-J. Gignoux, *L'Economie française entre les deux guerres, 1919-1939* (Paris: Société d'éditions économiques et sociales, 1942) and Shepard B. Clough, "Retardative Factors in French Economic Development," *The Tasks of Economic History*, Supplement VI, 1946 (papers of the Economic History Association, published as a supplement to the *Journal of Economic History*). Frank A. Haight, *A History of French Commercial Policies* (New York: Macmillan Co., 1941) is the standard work in English in its field.

For the 1920's, see W. Ogburn and W. Jaffe, *The Economic Development of Post-War France* (New York: Columbia University Press, 1929). H. W. Arndt, *The Economic Lessons of the Nineteen-Thirties* (London: Oxford University Press, 1944) has a section on France; the appropriate chapters in H. V. Hodson, *Slump and Recovery, 1929-1937* (London: Oxford University Press, 1938) show a better grasp of the French situation. A good discussion of the Great Depression in France is Bertrand Nogaro, *La Crise économique dans le monde et en France* (Paris: Librairie générale de droit et de jurisprudence, 1936). For a study of the effects of the Popular Front in one region of France, see André Braun, *L'Ouvrier al-*

sacien et l'expérience du front populaire (Paris: Recueil Sirey, 1938). The Ministry of Finance has published the *Bilan économique des cinq premiers mois du plan de trois ans* (Paris: Imprimerie Nationale, 1939) and *Mouvement économique en France de 1929 à 1939* (Paris: Imprimerie Nationale, 1941).

French financial institutions.—A good description of the French banking system is Henry Laufenburger, *Les Banques françaises* (Paris: Recueil Sirey, 1940). The standard work on the Bank of France to 1919 is Gabriel Ramon, *Histoire de la Banque de France* (Paris: Bernard Grasset, 1929). See also A. Dauphin-Meunier, *La Banque de France* (Paris: Gallimard, 1937). A useful introduction to the French money-market is Margaret Myers, *Paris as a Financial Centre* (New York: Columbia University Press, 1936) and Robert M. Haig, *The Public Finances of Post-War France* (New York: Columbia University Press, 1929). In the useful little *Collection Armand Colin* the foremost authority on French public finances, Louis Trotabas, has given us *Les Finances publiques et les impôts en France* (Paris: Armand Colin, 1937). For a description of the Exchange Stabilization Fund, see V. Polejina, *Les Fonds d'égalisation des changes* (Paris: Bossuet, 1939). The difficult task of explaining the operations of the forward exchange market is accomplished in Paul Einzig, *The Theory of Forward Exchange* (London: Macmillan Co., 1937). The effect of French capital movements on the London money-market is explained in Leonard Waight, *The History and Mechanism of the Exchange Equalisation Account* (Cambridge: Cambridge University Press, 1939).

French monetary policy and the franc.—The work of the late Professor Gaëtan Pirou is outstanding in this field. The material in his two small books *La Monnaie française depuis la guerre, 1914-1936* and *La Monnaie française de 1936 à 1938* (Paris: Recueil Sirey, 1936 and 1938) is repeated in his large work *Traité d'économie politique*, Vol. II, *Le Mécanisme de la vie économique: La Monnaie* (Paris: Recueil Sirey, 1945), perhaps the best single volume in any language on the history of money in the nineteenth and twentieth centuries. Georges Lachapelle, *Les Finances de la IIIᵉᵐᵉ République* (Paris: Flammarion, 1937) denounces the French for mishandling their financial problems. George Peel, *The Financial Crisis of France* and *The Economic Policy of France* (London: Macmillan Co., 1925 and 1937) are both rather shallow treatments, as is René Sédillot, *Histoire du franc* (Paris: Recueil Sirey, 1939) which devotes a few chapters to the modern era.

Three excellent American monographs deal with the French franc before 1929. They are Eleanor L. Dulles, *The French Franc, 1914-1928* (New York: Macmillan and Co., 1929); Haig, *The Public Finances of Post-War France*, cited above; and James H. Rogers, *The Process of Inflation in France, 1914-1927* (New York: Columbia University Press, 1929). See also Gaston Jèze, "The Economic and Financial Position of France in 1920," *Quarterly Journal of Economics*, February, 1921; Gaston Jèze and Henri Truchy, *The War Finances of France* ("Economic and Social History of the World War," Carnegie Endowment for International Peace, New Haven: Yale University Press, 1927); and, in the same series, Etienne Clémentel, *La France et la politique économique interalliée* (Paris: Presses Universitaires, 1931). For the aftermath of the war, see Albert Aftalion, "*Les expériences monétaires récentes et la théorie quantitative,*" *Revue d'économie politique,* 1925; the League of Nations monograph, *The Course and Control of Inflation* (Princeton: Princeton University Press, 1946); André Bouton, *La Fin des rentiers* (Paris: Editions M. P. Trémois, 1930); and the famous *Rapport du comité des experts* (Paris: Imprimerie Nationale, 1926). In Charles Rist, *Essais sur quelques problèmes économiques et monétaires* (Paris: Recueil Sirey, 1933), there are two chapters on the problem of monetary stabilization under the Poincaré régime. See also F. Lacombe, *Les Conséquences de la stabilisation monétaire française au point de vue des finances publiques* (Paris: E. Sagot et Cie., 1929), and William A. Brown, Jr., *The International Gold Standard Reinterpreted, 1914-1934,* 2 Vols. (New York: National Bureau of Economic Research, Inc., 1940).

For the years between the administrations of Poincaré and Blum we have a sort of financial autobiography by Germain-Martin, who was minister of finance or minister of the budget through most of this period, *Le Problème financier, 1930-1936* (Paris: Domat-Montchrestien, 1936). W. H. Wynne, "The French Franc, June, 1928-February, 1937," *Journal of Political Economy,* August, 1937, deals with the gold reserves problem. See also Paul Einzig, *France's Crisis* (London: Macmillan Co., 1934); P. Belgrand, *De la dévaluation de 1928 à la dévaluation de 1936* (Paris: Domat-Montchrestien, 1937); and G. Lacout and G. Damougeot-Perron, *Le Franc devant la crise* (Paris: Payot, 1934). Seymour E. Harris, *Exchange Depreciation, Its Theory and Its History, 1931-1935* (Cambridge: Harvard University Press, 1936) deals with the international race for cheap money and its consequences. Gustav Cassel discusses the role of France in the gold bloc in *The Downfall of the Gold Standard* (Oxford: Clarendon Press, 1936). In this connection, see also Albert Aftalion, *L'Or et sa distribution mondiale* (Paris: Dalloz, 1932). Olivier Wormser, *Déflation et Dévaluation, étude comparée de leurs effets sur les prix* (Paris: Recueil Sirey, 1938) is especially valuable for this period.

For two viewpoints on why the Blum experiments failed, see M. Kalecki, "The Lesson of the Blum Experiment," *The Economic Journal,* March, 1938, and Robert Marjolin, "Reflections on the Blum Experiment," *Economica,* May, 1938. Also useful for this period is Mehmet Mazhar, *La Dévaluation de la monnaie française de septembre 1936 et les circonstances qui l'ont amenée* (Paris: F. Loviton et Cie., 1937); A. Dumora, *La Réforme de la Banque de France et l'évolution monétaire de juin 1936 à juin 1937* (Bordeaux: Imprimeries Delmas, 1939); L.-R. De Couet, *Le Franc français postérieurement à septembre 1936* (Paris: Librairie sociale et économique, 1939); a brochure issued by the Institut d'études et d'informations économiques, *Le Front populaire et le contrôle des changes* (Paris,

1937) ; and O. Moreau-Néret, *Le Contrôle des prix en France* (Paris: Recueil Sirey, 1941). Important speeches on monetary policies can be found in the following brochures, mainly reprinted from the *Journal Officiel:* Raymond Poincaré, *La Restauration financière de la France* (Paris: Payot, 1928) ; Vincent Auriol, *Un Bilan, un programme, des actes* (Paris: Librairie Populaire, 1936) ; Léon Blum, *L'Exercice du Pouvoir* (Paris: Gallimard, 1937) ; Jacques Duclos, *La Dévaluation* (Paris: Editions du comité populaire de propagande, 1936) ; Paul Reynaud, *Sauver le régime et le pays* (Paris: Imprimerie Nationale, 1939) and *Courage de la France* (Paris: Flammarion, 1939).

For the last few years before World War II the following works are useful: P.-B. Vigreux, *De la monnaie à l'économie en France (1933-1938)* (Paris: Librairie générale de droit et de jurisprudence, 1938) ; F. Moliexe, *Le Système monétaire français (son évolution depuis 1936)* (Paris: Jouve et Cie., 1942) ; M. Mitzakis, *Principaux aspects de l'évolution financière de la France, 1936-1944* (Paris: Les publications techniques, 1944) ; and Charles Rist, "The Financial Situation of France," *Foreign Affairs*, July, 1938.

INDEX

Advances, Bank of France, 26, 29, 35-36, 53, 62-63, 132-133, 165-166, 168, 178, 193-194
"Attack on the franc," 33-35, 69
"Auriol franc," 146
Auriol, Vincent, 48, 138, 140-141, 145-146, 148, 173

Balances of payments, 155, 218; commodity trade, 27n, 57, 95-96, 126, 188; current balances, 58, 59, 93-96, 149-150, 189 (*see also* Capital movements; Gold movements)
Bank deposits, 18, 26n, 63, 100, 118, 194-195
Bank of England, 28, 48, 99
Bank of France, 14-16, 71, 98-99; discount policy (*bons*), 36, 113-114, 117-118, 166; discount rate, 34, 41, 61, 102, 117, 186; foreign exchange reserves, 47, 59-60, 98; influence in politics, 43n, 112, 141, 197; reform of, 141-142
Banking system, 16-17
Bloc National, 34, 35
Blum, Léon, 48, 138, 145, 180
Bond Defense Fund, 176
Bonds, long-term (*rentes*), 37, 49n, 51, 61, 116
Bonds, short-term (*bons*), 20, 45, 46, 60-61, 112, 116, 168-169 (*see also* Bank of France, discount policy)
"Bonnet franc," 175
Bonnet, Georges, 80, 109, 173
Briand, Aristide, 38
Budgetary equilibrium, 78-79, 82-83, 103-104, 105-106, 134
Budgets, 75, 77-78, 82, 107, 111, 150-151, 153, 176-177
"*Budgets extraordinaires*," 30, 150
Business cycles, 50n, 67, 86, 120-121, 154 (*see also* Depression)

Caillaux, Joseph, 22, 37, 42, 43
Caisse d'amortissement, 45-46, 52, 76
Capital movements, 57-58, 59-60, 185, 189-190 (*see also* "Hot money")
Cartel des Gauches, 35, 36, 43
Chautemps, Camille, 173, 176, 180
Committee of Experts, of 1926, 41-42; of 1933, 109; of 1937, 153, 156

Communist party, 44, 114, 138, 145
Convertibility, 25, 52, 147, 153
Cost of living, 55, 93, 125, 159, 192
Crédit National, 16, 30, 34

Daladier, Edouard, 181, 182, 183
Dawes Committee, 31-32
Decree-laws, 42, 110, 112, 114-115, 169, 173, 181, 208-209
"Declaration of Rambouillet," 178-179
Deflation, 131-134; abandonment of, 118-119, 139, 203; deflationary measures, 115; theory of, 106-107, 110, 135-137, 202
Depreciation of the franc, 26-27, 28 (*see also* Dollar rate in Paris; Sterling rate in Paris)
Depression, of 1920-1921, 28, 53; of 1929, lag in France, 73, 84-86, 88-90, 95, 199-200; of 1937-1938, 190
Devaluation, American, 99-100, 127; Belgian, 109n, 114; British 99, 127
Devaluation of the franc, of 1926 (stabilization), 46-47; of 1928, 49, 51, 52; of 1936, 145-147; of 1937, 175; of 1938, 181-182
Dollar rate in Paris, 27, 66, 102, 157, 213
Doumergue, Gaston, 109-112

"Elastic franc," 146, 163
Employment, 56, 92, 121, 144, 151, 161-162
Exchange control, 26-28, 147-148, 170, 195
Exchange Equalisation Account (British), 154, 163n, 190
Exchange rate, *see* Dollar rate in Paris; Sterling rate in Paris
Exchange Stabilization Fund (French), 147, 152, 153, 156, 164, 168, 174, 178, 179, 190

February 6 riots (1934), 129
Financial panics, 81, 101, 156, 183; London panic of Sept., 1931, 80, 99
Fiscal year, 76-77, 82
Flandin, Pierre-Étienne, 112-114
"Flight from the franc," 39-41, 43, 67-68, 198
Floating debt, 40, 60-61, 168-169